The How-To Book of Catholic Theology

Nihil Obstat
Msgr. Michael Heintz, Ph.D.
Censor Librorum

Imprimatur
✠ Kevin C. Rhoades
Bishop of Fort Wayne-South Bend
June 21, 2020

The *Nihil Obstat* and *Imprimatur* are official declarations that a book is free from doctrinal or moral error. It is not implied that those who have granted the *Nihil Obstat* and *Imprimatur* agree with the contents, opinions, or statements expressed.

The How-To Book of

Catholic
Theology

Everything
You Need to
Know but No
One Ever
Taught You

Fr. John P. Cush, S.T.D.

In gratitude to the Most Reverend Nicholas DiMarzio, Ph.D., D.D., Bishop of Brooklyn, who encouraged me to study, to teach, and to write as a diocesan priest

Contents

Introduction   9

1. Who Is a Theologian?   13

2. What Do I Need to Do to Start My Study of Theology?   33

3. Why Are There So Many "Ologies"?   43

4. How Do I Form a Theological Method?   55

5. How Do I Use the "Tools" of Theology —
   Sacred Scripture and Sacred Tradition?
   Some Personal Examples   65

6. A Brief History of Theology   97

7. How Does the Study of Theology
   Lead to Holiness of Life?   127

8. Toward a Spirituality of Study   155

Postscript   167

Acknowledgments   169

Appendix One
Some Suggestions for Building a Catholic Library   173

Appendix Two
Building a Library of Catholic Spiritual Classics   181

Appendix Three
Building a Library of Catholic Fiction   193

Appendix Four
Building a Library of the Fiction Classics
of Western Civilization   203

Notes   211

Introduction

Let's begin with a prayer.

> Father, may everything we do begin with your inspiration and continue with your saving help. Let our work always find its origin in you and through you reach completion. We ask this through Christ our Lord.[1]

I really blame my teachers in grade school. When I was a small boy growing up in the Windsor Terrace section of Brooklyn, I went to the local Catholic school, Holy Name of Jesus (now known as Saint Joseph the Worker Catholic Academy). It was right down the block from where my family lived over Farrell's Bar, one of the most famous pubs in all of New York City. I went to Holy Name from kindergarten to eighth grade (1977–1986, so you can imagine how ancient I am now). It was an interesting time in the history of the Church, those early Pope Saint John Paul II years. One of my earliest memories of Mass is a rousing guitar version of "Peace Is Flowing Like a River," which we sang as first graders at a school Mass. It was a time when many traditional practices were left behind, with nothing offered in their place. For instance, the first time I experienced exposition and Benediction of the Most

Blessed Sacrament was when I entered the minor seminary. For the most part, it was a bland, whitewashed period for the Catholic Church in the United States.

Beyond the principal and the sister who taught art to all grades, we had no presence of religious women in the classrooms. We were, however, blessed with two very fine Xaverian brothers in the upper grades. Our classes were otherwise taught by younger laywomen, and in the sixth and seventh grades two of them were the very first persons to ask me to consider a priestly vocation. As an obedient young man (who had a massive crush on one of the teachers and would have done anything she asked), I really thought about it and wanted to learn more.

When the time came to apply to high school, there was really only one choice for me: Cathedral Preparatory Seminary in Elmhurst, Queens. A freestanding day school, Cathedral was the perfect high school for me. The Diocese of Brooklyn is still blessed to have a cathedral school, now known as Cathedral Preparatory School and Seminary. It was at Cathedral that I met some of the finest priests (and people) I have known. Inspired by daily Mass, adoration of the Most Blessed Sacrament, retreats, spiritual direction, a great classical education (lots of Latin and history), and, perhaps most importantly, the daily presence of diocesan priests in the classroom and in all areas of student life, I felt even more strongly a call to explore the vocation. When people ask me what I did before I entered the seminary, I tell them that I was in eighth grade. I am a "lifer" when it comes to my seminary formation (and proud of it!). Later, for eight happy years of my priesthood, I was assigned to teach at Cathedral Prep, and it was one of the best experiences of my life.

For my college years, I went to Cathedral Residence of the Immaculate Conception in Douglaston, Queens (now known as Cathedral Seminary House of Formation, a minor seminary and pretheologate for the Archdiocese of New York and the Dioceses of Brooklyn, Rockville Centre, Scranton, Albany, and a few others), while earning my bachelor's degree in philosophy and English at St. John's University. Afterwards, I was asked to study for the priesthood in Rome at the Pontifical North American College.

The North American College (or NAC, as some call it) was a wonderful experience of priestly formation. Our rector, then Monsignor (now Archbishop and Cardinal) Timothy Dolan, and his faculty were stunning examples of the priesthood, and the formation that we received was top-notch. When people ask me if I have read Cardinal Dolan's book *Priests for the Third Millennium*, I tell them that I have lived it. Currently, I am honored to serve on the formation faculty of the North American College as the academic dean and as a formation advisor; I am also a professor of theology and US Catholic Church history.

It was in Rome that I truly fell in love with theology and the great traditions of the Church. I grew to love both the study of theology as an academic field and the application of theology to the daily life of the Church. Having been blessed to have been assigned to complete both a license and a doctorate in sacred theology in the field of fundamental theology at the Pontifical Gregorian University in Rome, I can tell you that studying theology has truly changed my life as a person, as a Catholic believer, and as a priest. For me, theology isn't an esoteric, abstract subject. It's talking about someone I love — Jesus — and his Church. It is my hope to explain in this book the connection between theology and life. As a priest and a theologian, I am excited to be with you on this journey as I try to fulfill Christ's command "*docete omnes gentes*," or "make disciples of all nations" (Mt 28:19).

At the end of most chapters, I have included a "Suggestions for Further Reading" section, in case you would like to investigate further some of the concepts introduced in this text. At the end of the book, there are several appendixes listing works to help the prospective theologian build up his or her library, along with my reflections on the works.

1

Who Is a Theologian?

I magine you've fallen in love with a beautiful woman (or a handsome man). You want to spend your time getting to know all about her. You want to know what she knows, what she thinks, and why. You want to know all about her history: Where did she grow up? What's her family like?

Just as this is the case when love begins between a man and a woman, so it is in our spiritual lives with God. If you are reading this book, perhaps you have already fallen in love with a Person — a Divine Person with two natures, human and divine. Of course, this Divine Person is Jesus Christ our Lord. If you have fallen in love with the Lord Jesus, you want to know all about him. You want to know his life story (which we can find in Sacred Scripture). You want to know what he thinks and about his history — which is continued beyond Scripture, in the lived experience of the Body of Christ (which is his Church), that is found in Sacred Tradition. You want to know all about the Lord, who is our God. And it is this God himself who is the subject of theology.

What Have I Gotten Myself Into?

You may be agreeing with me right now and saying to yourself that you have indeed fallen in love with Love itself, Jesus Christ. You may be thinking that you do want to know all about Jesus and the Church. You may be realizing that you want to know more about your faith. You may have noticed so many others speaking about this word "theology." And yet there might be a huge stumbling block: "I really don't know what theology is!"

The term "theology" can sound so very technical, and yet the truth of the matter is that it is quite simple — and it needs to be! Theology does include many technical terms — Christology, eschatology, pneumatology, etc. — that are important concepts to know, and we will get to them. (If you're impatient and want to read ahead a bit, chapter three gives definitions for all these "ologies.") But the primary focus of this book is the *fundamentals of theology* — that is, the most basic questions that may be on your mind if you are reading this: What is theology? How do I go about "doing" theology? How can I reconcile differing theological opinions and approaches? How does the teaching office of the Church, which we call the Magisterium, shape my study? And how does personal holiness lead to good theology and vice versa?

These are all great questions, and we will cover each of them in this book. For this chapter, however, I want to explore two preliminary questions: *What is theology?* and *What do I need to know before I can begin to do theology?* I also want to offer you a little bit of reassurance as we begin this study: I can pretty much guarantee that you are, in many ways, a theologian already. What kind of theologian? Good question! Bear with me as we take a closer look.

Before we go any further, I want to speak about models. No, not runway models ... and no, not the ones you need glue to construct or that you can fit into a bottle. What I mean is models, or styles, of being a theologian. In his book *Retrieving Fundamental*

Theology: The Three Styles of Contemporary Theology,[1] a theologian who taught me as a seminarian many years ago, Father Gerald O'Collins, SJ, offers a helpful way of looking at theology. Father O'Collins says that there are three types of theologians — three models, if you will, or styles of doing theology: the academic, the pastoral, and the spiritual.

The first is an academic model, that of the theologian who is formally trying to figure out the great and deep questions of life. We can call this the "theologian in the classroom." The second model is the "theologian in the streets" — the man or woman of faith who is most concerned with bringing the faith that they have, and the theology that they have studied, into the direct pastoral service of God's people. This is the theologian who is a pastor — the theologian involved in an apostolate who may not be interested in creating a complex, systematic theology textbook. The third model is the "theologian in the chapel." This is the one who may not be creating a complex, systematic theology and is not necessarily active in the world, but is praying to God — this is the one who, by his or her life, offers a lesson in theology simply by being a man or woman of faith.

Let's take a look at some of the theologians and saints throughout Church history and see what they might offer us as examples to follow in our study of theology. How are all these theologians different? What do they all have in common? How can they help us to become better theologians?

The Theologian in the Classroom — *"Fides Quaerens Intellectum"*

The first type is the academic theologian, the one whom we've called the "theologian in the classroom." This is the professor, the one who systematically investigates the mysteries of the faith and exemplifies the adage that theology is *"fides quaerens intellectum,"* or "faith seeking understanding," as Saint Anselm of Canterbury described it. I'll use Saint Anselm himself as an example of an academic theologian.

Saint Anselm of Canterbury

The great Saint Anselm of Canterbury (1033/4–1109) was the one who first described theology as "*fides quaerens intellectum.*" Saint Anselm was a Benedictine monk who was born in Italy. In the course of living his monastic vocation, he was appointed to serve as the abbot of the monastery at Bec, France, before going to England, not long after the Norman Conquest, to become the archbishop of Canterbury. Saint Anselm wanted to understand the faith in which he believed and to communicate that faith rationally to the world. He wrote: "As I see it, it is a sign of slackness, when once we have found the faith, to make no effort to understand what we believe."[2]

> **As I see it, it is a sign of slackness, when once we have found the faith, to make no effort to understand what we believe.**
> (Saint Anselm)

My first encounter with Saint Anselm was in an undergraduate philosophy class at St. John's University in New York. Our professor, Father Robert Lauder, a great teacher and a diocesan priest (whom I later took on as my spiritual director when I was discerning my own vocation), emphasized not only Saint Anselm's *intellectum* (intellect) but also his tremendous *fides* (faith). Since that time, I have taken this great abbot as a special patron for my own studies as a priest in philosophy and theology. I am grateful to Saint Anselm — his intercession has helped me get through many years of study. And I know that if you call on his help, he'll answer you!

Saint Anselm was a true monk who rooted all of his theology in prayer; even his famous "proof for the existence of God" — which can be summed up as "God is a being than which none greater can be conceived" — was originally written not as a theological text but as a prayer. He combined deep, contemplative prayer (his own faith) with study (his intellect) in order to grapple with some of the most difficult questions of the faith. These questions include why it is reasonable to believe in God, which he discusses in his work the *Proslogion* (Discourse on the Existence of God); and why God took on flesh — his work *Cur Deus Homo* (Why God Became Man) explains how God's divine love, responding to human rebelliousness, requires that God should become a human being.

Have you ever thought about questions such as the reasonableness of believing in a God whom we cannot see, or why God the Son became incarnate, taking on flesh in this world? If so, you might find Saint Anselm a helpful friend and example!

In his preface to the *Proslogion*, Saint Anselm describes how he approaches his work as a theologian:

> I have written the little work that follows ... in the role of one who strives to raise his mind to the contemplation of God and one who seeks to understand what he believes.
>
> I acknowledge, Lord, and I give thanks that you have created your image in me, so that I may remember you, think of you, love you. But this image is so obliterated and worn away by wickedness, it is so obscured by the smoke of sins, that it cannot do what it was created to do, unless you renew and reform it. I am not attempting, O Lord, to penetrate your loftiness, for I cannot begin to match my understanding with it, but I desire in some measure to understand your truth, which my heart believes and loves. For I do not seek to understand in order that I may believe, but I believe in order to understand. For this too I believe, that "unless I believe, I shall not

understand" (Isa. 7:9).[3]

> *For this too I believe, that "unless*
> *I believe, I shall not understand."*
> (Saint Anselm)

Notice that for Saint Anselm, faith leads to understanding; there is no opposition between the two. He knows that God is God, that he is not, and that this is perfectly okay! But his faith leads to a greater desire to understand — a desire to know the Lord Jesus that can only come from prayer and study.

The Theologian in the Streets *Pastoral*

The second type of theologian is the pastoral theologian, the "theologian in the streets." This is someone who takes his or her study of theology and uses it to try to actively engage the People of God in an attempt to make the faith accessible. This is one who, having studied the mysteries of the faith, tries to bring that faith to the world and exemplifies the adage often attributed to Saint Francis of Assisi: "Preach the Gospel always; use words when necessary." Recall that many of the Fathers of the Church were not academic theologians teaching in a classroom but pastors preaching and responding to the needs and concerns of their people.

Dorothy Day — *"Deo Gratias!"*

Servant of God Dorothy Day (1897–1980) is an example of a "theologian in the streets" — one whose theology is based on the lived experience of God's love and the desire to love God through service to his people in need.

I first got to know the works of Dorothy Day through my philosophy professor at St. John's University, Father Robert Lauder, whom I've already mentioned above. He invited us to come with him when he gave a talk on Catholic novels to the Manhattan

Catholic Worker group. It was a profound night that changed my life by exposing me to one of the most important American Roman Catholics and the great work that she did.

Dorothy Day, born in Brooklyn, New York, in 1897, lived a radical life. In her college years, she became influenced by socialist and anarchist ideals. Living a rather bohemian lifestyle, she had an abortion and then a child out of wedlock. Gradually, she began to explore Catholicism and, through Mass attendance, spiritual reading, and devotions, began to discover the beauty of the Faith. She had her infant daughter, Tamar, baptized and became more and more involved in her faith.

This involvement with her faith enkindled a desire for activism. She met Peter Maurin, a former Christian Brother[4] who fell away from the Faith, became involved with communism and socialism, and then returned to the Catholic Faith. Maurin had a love for the poor and a desire for social justice similar to that of Day — but unlike her, he had a deep knowledge of the official social teachings of the Church, a love for the Fathers of the Church, a deep knowledge of Scholastic theology, and a devotion to the philosophy of Christian personalism. Dorothy Day's uncompromising love for the poor and her desire to better the world through Catholic social teaching, combined with Maurin's background in theology, helped to launch the Catholic Worker movement, a force for good for the poor in the world that exists to this day. In her work *From Union Square to Rome* (1938), she writes:

> I had a conversation with John Spivak, the Communist writer, a few years ago, and he said to me, "How can you believe? How can you believe in the Immaculate Conception, in the Virgin birth, in the Resurrection?" I could only say that I believe in the Roman Catholic Church and all she teaches. I have accepted Her authority with my whole heart. At the same time, I want to point out to you

that we are taught to pray for final perseverance. We are taught that faith is a gift, and sometimes I wonder why some have it and some do not. I feel my own unworthiness and can never be grateful enough to God for His gift of faith.[5]

> *We are taught that faith is a gift, and sometimes I wonder why some have it and some do not. I feel my own unworthiness and can never be grateful enough to God for His gift of faith.*
> (Dorothy Day)

The epitaph on Day's tombstone is the same as that of Saint Cyprian of Carthage, one of the great Fathers of the Church — "*Deo Gratias!*" — which means, "Thanks be to God!"

Dorothy Day possessed tremendous faith in Christ and his Church and a desire to know more about that faith in order to serve others. She, as a "theologian in the streets," embodies what it means — having come to know God through faith and prayer — to serve God's people in the world. Her knowledge of God through study and her great love of God and the Church led her to say, "*Deo Gratias!*"

The Theologian in the Chapel — spiritual Encountering God in Prayer

The third type of theologian is the spiritual theologian, the "theologian in the chapel," someone who uses his or her study of theology to deepen his or her relationship with Christ. This is one who, having studied the mysteries of the Faith, tries to bring that theology into his or her dialogue with the beloved, Jesus. This can be exemplified by the adage attributed to Saint Prosper of Aquitaine (c. 390–c. 455), "*lex orandi, lex credendi,*" meaning the "law of prayer is the law of belief."[6]

Thérèse of Lisieux — Her "Little Way"

One example of a "theologian in the chapel" from recent Catholic tradition is the great female Doctor of the Church, Saint Thérèse of Lisieux (1873–1897), also known as the Little Flower. When Pope Saint John Paul II gave her this appellation in 1997, one priest I know — who at that time was in graduate school studying complex biblical theology — was furious. "Her complete dogmatic theological corpus could fit on the back of a postage stamp!" he sputtered. And indeed, she is not a systematic theologian — yet Thérèse is nonetheless a great theologian, for she continually sought to deepen her relationship (and ours) with the Lord.[7] In my room at the seminary, I have a statue of my dear, dear friend, the Little Flower, right next to one of Our Lady, Seat of Wisdom. Thérèse is, for me, a continual font of wisdom, and not a day goes by that I don't ask her intercession.

Thérèse Martin was born to a couple, Louis and Zélie Martin, who themselves were eventually canonized as saints. Feeling the call to religious life, she wanted to enter the Carmelite convent at Lisieux as a girl but was too young to do so. After appealing directly to Pope Leo XIII while on pilgrimage in Rome, she was permitted to take the veil at the age of fifteen.

Thérèse's time at the Carmel was not without challenges (she struggled with spiritual dryness and desolation, and she wanted to go to the missions, but poor health prevented her from doing so), yet she nevertheless sought to grow in the way of perfection. Through her way of life and through her own writings, collected as *The Story of a Soul*, Saint Thérèse is a shining example of one who is not, and never would have dared to consider herself, a systematic theologian, but who is truly a Doctor of the Church. Her "little way" of growing in holiness has taught more people about the Catholic Faith than the writings of more complex thinkers. She found and lived her faith in Jesus, and her wisdom is every bit as profound as the academic theologian's. This young nun writes in her autobiography:

> I understand and I know from experience that: "The
> kingdom of God is within you." Jesus has no need of
> books or teachers to instruct souls; He teaches without
> the noise of words. Never have I heard Him speak, but
> I feel that He is within me at each moment; He is guid-
> ing and inspiring me with what I must say and do. I find
> just when I need them certain lights that I had not seen
> until then, and it isn't most frequently during my hours
> of prayer that these are most abundant but rather in the
> midst of my daily occupations.[8]

> ***Jesus has no need of books or teachers
> to instruct souls; He teaches without the noise of
> words. Never have I heard Him speak, but I feel that
> He is within me at each moment;
> He is guiding and inspiring me with what
> I must say and do.***
> (Saint Thérèse of Lisieux)

Even though she never left her Carmel, Thérèse's pastoral theology is as profound as that of any social activist. Read her experience and wisdom, even as a young lady, of her growth in humility
and charity:

> Another time I was working in the laundry, and the
> Sister opposite, while washing handkerchiefs, repeated-
> ly splashed me with dirty water. My first impulse was
> to draw back and wipe my face, to show the offender I
> should be glad if she would behave more quietly; but the
> next minute I thought how foolish it was to refuse the
> treasures God offered me so generously, and I refrained

from betraying my annoyance. On the contrary, I made such efforts to welcome the shower of dirty water, that at the end of half an hour I had taken quite a fancy to this novel kind of aspersion, and I resolved to come as often as I could to the happy spot where such treasures were freely bestowed.[9]

The Little Flower died at the age of twenty-four in 1897; soon after, a devotion to her grew in France and spread quickly throughout the world. Thérèse was canonized in 1925 and was made the universal copatron of the missions in 1927. In the booklet for her declaration as a Doctor of the Church in 1997, the Vatican declared: "On the occasion of the centenary of her death, many Episcopal Conferences have asked the Pope to declare her a Doctor of the Church, in view of the soundness of her spiritual wisdom inspired by the Gospel, the originality of her theological intuitions filled with sublime teaching, and the universal acceptance of her spiritual message, which has been welcomed throughout the world and spread by the translation of her works into over fifty languages."[10]

Not bad for a twenty-four-year-old Carmelite nun to stand alongside such theological masters as Augustine, Gregory the Great, and Thomas Aquinas!

Principles of Sound Theology

Can you see yourself in any of these categories?

- Do you like to study about your faith, pick up a book and read, perhaps the *Catechism of the Catholic Church*, trying to figure out what exactly the Church teaches and why?
- Do your study and prayer lead you to see Christ in all people and want to serve them as Christ serves?

- Do your reading and study lead you to prayer, to deep contemplation, to wanting to spend even more time with the Lord?

If any of these describe you, then guess what? You have the makings of a really good theologian! The key is to figure out how to be a theologian in the classroom without becoming too academic, a theologian in the streets without becoming too much of an activist, and a theologian in the chapel without growing too far apart from the world. It's all about balance.

So What Do Saint Anselm, Dorothy Day, and the Little Flower Have in Common?

What do all three types of theologians have in common? They each demonstrate valid ways of "doing theology." To understand what we mean by "doing theology," we need to examine the very root of the word "theology." If we break the word up, we find two Greek words — *theos*, meaning "God," and *logos*, meaning "reason or word" — so at its essence, theology is the study of God's word. However, we need to recall that by the phrase "God's word," we mean much more than just Sacred Scripture. We mean God's Word Incarnate, our Lord and Savior, Jesus.

Doing theology, then, is studying and learning about, praying to, and then teaching about the one we love, who loves us. It is about encountering God's self-revelation in Christ through the Church, a self-revelation that includes both Sacred Scripture and Sacred Tradition — in other words, what we call wisdom. As Saint Paul wrote to the Corinthians: "It is due to him [God] that you are in Christ Jesus, who became for us wisdom from God, as well as righteousness, sanctification, and redemption" (1 Cor 1:30, NABRE). It is in Christ that we find wisdom. It is through Christ that we are entirely redeemed and transformed — body, mind, and spirit. As we read in the Letter of Saint Paul to the Romans, as we offer ourselves to

God, we will be transformed by the renewal of our minds, that we "may discern what is the will of God, what is good and pleasing and perfect" (Rom 12:1–2, NABRE).

How, then, do we begin? Well, the most important tool that you will need to study God is not something you can acquire for yourself, or see, or touch. You can't find it in a library or buy it in a bookstore. The single most important part of being a theologian is ...

You Have to Have *Faith*

I cannot emphasize enough the absolute necessity of being a person of faith and the absolute necessity of a personal and ecclesial adherence to the Person of Jesus Christ if one wishes to study theology successfully. If you think about it, what did Saint Anselm, Dorothy Day, and the Little Flower have in common? They were all Catholics who believed in Christ and his Church and practiced their faith.

I could study every single detail about the Muslim religion, I could know its history, I could explain its practices, I could have academic degrees in all sorts of relevant fields from all sorts of universities; however, I still wouldn't be a Muslim theologian. Why? It's pretty simple: I don't believe in the Muslim religion; I do not adhere to its practices or hold its tenets. At best, all I would be is a historian of the religion.

The theologian must be a person of faith.

The theologian must be a person of faith. He or she must believe in what he or she studies and teaches. He or she must worship the subject of his or her study, and for a Christian, that subject is Christ Jesus. And a Catholic theologian must do so within the Church.

One must believe in God, in Christ, and in the Church in order to be a Catholic theologian. Father Aidan Nichols, OP, explains this well in his work *The Shape of Catholic Theology*: "What, then, is this faith which is so imperative for the theologian? It can be thought of in two ways: either as the body of belief which the Church, the Christian community, holds to be true, or as my own personal act of faith, my very own act of believing adhesion to God in Christ by the Holy Spirit."[11]

Father Nichols is getting at a theological distinction: Faith involves both a *fides qua creditur* ("faith by which something is believed" — the act of believing) and a *fides quae creditur* ("faith which is believed" — matters of doctrine). It involves my own act of belief in Christ as well as the Church's adherence to the truths he has revealed in her. The two aspects of believing are not opposed to each other. It's not as if we must choose one or the other. To do so would be false and create an unnatural dualism.

Another way to refer to this is to speak about the subjective and the objective aspects of faith. The subjective aspect of faith is the aspect of faith by which we, as individuals, choose to embrace the truth offered to us in the Church's teachings. This does not mean I engage in a "subjective" picking and choosing regarding what I myself want to believe. Rather, the *fides qua* is that faith by which the individual accepts the objective faith of the Church herself; and this subjective act of faith by the individual always occurs with and in God, with and in the Blessed Trinity. The objective aspect of faith is the faith of the Church — that is, those truths of our Catholic faith that are clearly taught and that must be regarded as true. Remember the prayer that is titled "Acts of Faith, Hope, and Charity"? The Act of Faith is "My God, I believe in Thee, and all Thy Church doth teach, because Thou hast said it and Thy word is True."

To be a Catholic theologian is to embrace the teachings of the Church and to accept the freedom that comes from working within the boundaries established by the Church in her "rule of faith," which is taught from Divine Revelation (namely Sacred Scripture and Sacred Tradition) and in her clear, consistent Magisterium. We should have great confidence that the Church's *fides quae* will never fail, no matter what difficulties we might have in our own personal faith.

Understanding the Nonnegotiables

There are certain nonnegotiables that one must believe in order to be a Catholic theologian. The primary, or most basic, required beliefs are those taught in the Creed. Here are some examples:

- There is One God, with three Divine Persons in God.
- Through his Incarnation, the Second Person of the Most Blessed Trinity — Jesus — became like us in all things but sin. Jesus is One Divine Person with two natures, human and divine.
- The Holy Spirit is the "Lord and Giver of Life."
- The Blessed Mary is ever-Virgin and is the Immaculate Conception.
- There are seven sacraments — among them, baptism is entry to life in Christ, and the Eucharist is the true Body and Blood of the Lord.

These are the essential truths of the Faith, and the *Catechism of the Catholic Church* is a gift to us that clearly and consistently offers us the official, ecclesial understanding of these truths.

The Catholic theologian needs to have his natural academic interest enlightened by faith in God and in his Church. A Catholic theologian's theological orthodoxy, then, flows from his or her striving for faith and holiness as a member of Christ's Body, the People of God, the Church. Holiness of life leads to good theology.

Ressourcement (Return) and *Aggiornamento* (Renewal)

If we wish to be Catholic theologians, we must embrace Christ. The

Second Vatican Council brings us two guiding principles for doing so today. We must rediscover, with fresh eyes, the wellsprings of the Faith, including Sacred Scripture and the writings of the Fathers of the Church; the Second Vatican Council calls this return to the wellsprings, or the sources, *ressourcement* (a French word). We must also faithfully proclaim the Good News of Christ to the modern world in language both intelligible and pastorally welcoming; the term the Council uses for bringing the Gospel to the modern world is *aggiornamento* (an Italian word). Without *aggiornamento*, *ressourcement* can seem to be only a study of history; without a grounding in *ressourcement*, *aggiornamento* can seem to be merely an accommodation of the secular culture. We need both in order to do theology today, and we need an adherence to Jesus Christ as the source and center of our study.[12]

Believe in Christ and in the Church

In order to be theologians, we must believe in Christ. Otherwise, we're wasting our time. And our faith has to be practiced within the Church. We have to know the Church as our Mother and understand her as the spotless, sinless Bride of Christ. We know that while we who make up the Church are sinners, the Church is the Barque of Peter, traveling throughout salvation history, and this ship will never sink, for Christ is her pilot. The theologian sees the problems and anxieties, confusions, and need for clarification that exist in the Church and the world today, but he or she also has a sense of security. Our Mother, the Church, has been through it all before. Do you think things are confusing in the world of the twenty-first century? Do you think so many opinions and voices are being offered that no one really knows to whom in the Church they should listen? Imagine what it was like at the time of the Council of Nicaea, when people in the street were engaged in fisticuffs over theological issues involving Christ's divinity. God is in charge, and he is good, never allowing his Bride, the Church, to really sink. Have faith!

Beginning Formal Theological Study

A question that I am asked time and again when it comes to beginning the study of theology is, *What do I need to do to start my study?* What I always say to the prospective student is pretty simple: First, have faith in Christ and in his Church. And second, pray!

Good theology can arise only out of holiness of life.

Remember that, above all else, theology is the study of God and the things of God. It is not and cannot be the study of man exclusively. That's anthropology. To be sure, there can be a real and true theological anthropology, which would be the study of what it means to be a human being in light of God. But theology's starting point must be God and the things of God. Then, from that starting point in God, we can study everything else — from humanity, to creation, to every problem in the world.

What Theologians Should I Read?

You can trust the theology of someone who has the title "Saint" in front of his or her name. Good theology can arise only out of holiness of life. This is a truth that can be seen throughout history. Does this mean that we can't learn from modern and contemporary theologians? Of course not. In every age, the Church has raised up men and women who are able to teach the world new insights about the eternal message of the Good News. Throughout this book, I will mention several key Catholic theologians: men and women of faith, study, and service.

Are There Some Theologians I Should *Not* Read?

Well, that's a good question! We are living in an age where every single person with a laptop, the internet, and an idea to espouse can go online and become a "published theologian." The digital age — with blogs, forums, self-published e-books, and postings within the various social media — has created a whole new world where whosoever gets the most "hits" and "likes" seems to win a theological debate.

This is not a good thing. I am all for the open exchange of ideas, but one has to have a solid grounding on which to base his or her theological ideas. They cannot be based simply on opinions or personal preferences! The theologian should be a person of both faith and knowledge.

What Else Do I Have to Know?

Now, on to some practical things. A basic understanding of philosophy is needed in order to really understand theology. This may sound like a terrifying prospect, especially if you have ever had to take a class in philosophy that seemed like "navel-gazing" because the topics were far too abstract. But philosophy is essential: It is the handmaiden to theology. It provides theology with the concepts, the "skeleton," if you will, upon which we can hang our understanding of Divine Revelation.

Philosophy helps us to understand God, the human person, the world, and our relationships with them. Philosophy influences peoples and cultures. For example, some may not be able to identify a specific type of philosophy called relativism, yet many are relativistic in their attitudes and practice. In chapter three, we will discuss more fully how philosophy helps us in our understanding of theology.

Although the Church does not have an "official" philosophy, the perennial philosophy that comes from the thought of the great Doctor of the Church Saint Thomas Aquinas offers us the clearest and most realistic philosophy from which we can learn to "do" theology. Countless popes, from Leo XIII to Francis, have recommended that Saint Thomas's thought be the wisdom that guides our philosophical journey. Pope Leo XIII noted that Saint Thomas's theology was a definitive exposition of Catholic doctrine and directed clergy to adopt his thought as the basis of their theological positions. We will discuss why Saint Thomas is important for our study of theology in chapter two.

Theology Leads Us to the Sources

Once we have our bearings in faith and in philosophy, where should our study of theology take us? Truly Catholic theology begins first and foremost with the deposit of Divine Revelation, expressed first in Sacred Scripture and then in Sacred Tradition. Next, the subject is studied through the Magisterium of the Church. Only after these phases should speculative questions in theology come into play. Theology is traditionally studied through Sacred Scripture, then Sacred Tradition, then the Magisterium, and, finally, positive theology.[13]

In our next chapter, we will dive into some of the preliminary things we need to have down so we can study theology! But first, here are a few things to think and pray about concerning this chapter.

Points to Remember

- Theology is all about learning about and falling in love with the one who is Love itself, Jesus Christ our Lord.
- You must be a believer if you are to be a theologian.
- If you are a theologian, you must do it through, with, and in the Church.
- There are many different styles of being a theologian, some of which are more intellectual, others of which are more active, and yet others of which are more spiritual — but in order to be a good theologian, you

must be able to integrate all of them into your life as a Catholic Christian.

Suggestions for Further Reading

For further reading concerning topics in this chapter, you might want to consult the following:

- Robert Imbelli, *Rekindling the Christic Imagination: Theological Meditations for the New Evangelization* (Collegeville, MN: Liturgical Press, 2014), xiii–xx.
- Aidan Nichols, OP, *The Shape of Catholic Theology* (Edinburgh: T&T Clark, 1991), 13–41.
- Gerald O'Collins, SJ, *Rethinking Fundamental Theology* (New York: Oxford University Press, 2011), 322–41.
- Tracey Rowland, *Catholic Theology* (Edinburgh: T&T Clark, 2017).

2

What Do I Need to Do to Start My Study of Theology?

A s I mentioned in the last chapter, a question that I am asked time and again when it comes to beginning the study of theology is, *What do I need to do to start my study?* It is an important question with an important answer — so important that it bears repeating. What I always say to the prospective student is pretty simple: First, have faith in Christ and in his Church; second, pray; third, be a person of reason; and, fourth, place all of your study at the service of God and his Church.

Please remember that you are already a theologian if you ponder the great mystery that is God. This was an important insight from our first chapter. It is important to understand that the three styles of being a theologian — in the classroom, in the streets, and in the chapel — are certainly not in opposition to, but rather exist to complement, each other. The real theologian is a person of knowledge, of service, and of prayer.

Be a Person of Faith

It may sound all too simplistic, but the truth of the matter is, I think, straightforward: A theologian who does not have faith in Christ, who does not have faith in the Church that Christ founded, and who is not a prayerful person cannot be a Catholic theologian. At best, he would be a scholar of religious studies or a historian of religion. As we noted earlier, theology is, as Saint Anselm describes, "*fides quaerens intellectum*" — that is, "faith seeking understanding" (*Proslogion* II–IV).

The person who wishes to study theology must be a person of faith. It can't be a mere academic matter. It has to involve the desire to study someone whom we love, someone who has entered our life. Theology is all about studying a Person, a Divine Person with two natures, human and divine, a man like us in all things but sin, Jesus Christ the Lord. It is all about falling in love with him and with his Church.

What Does Faith Have to Do with Philosophy?

What does being a person of faith have to do with philosophy? The short answer is that God made us with an intellect, or mind, capable of knowing him and knowing truth. We use our mind when we study Scripture. We use it when we learn prayers. We use it in the very acts of belief that make us persons of faith. We use our mind every moment of every day! We use it for countless purposes, many of which don't have anything directly to do with the things of God. This is where various philosophies come in. Some philosophers observe that humans have minds, but they don't believe that humans are created by God; therefore, they come up with all kinds of philosophies to explain who humans are, what the world is, and where everything comes from. Other philosophers such as Saint Thomas Aquinas think humans can only have minds in the first place because we are made in the image of a Divine Person who himself has a Divine Mind. This type of philosophy walks hand in hand with the theology we have been describing because it thinks about everything that exists as originating in God.

Philosophy — Not *What* to Think, But *How* to Think

For several years, I taught classes in fundamental, dogmatic, liturgical, and spiritual theology to candidates for the permanent diaconate. I am very grateful that I was afforded this opportunity, because it helped me learn to be a professor of theology and also to communicate some key doctrinal ideas in a manner that was engaging and thorough, yet pastoral. There is a big difference between teaching theology to high school students and teaching theology to adult men who wish to be ordained for service in the Church. There is a massive distinction between *pedagogy* (teaching young people) and *andragogy* (teaching adults), a distinction that I had to learn pretty quickly as a professor.

One of the things that I came to recognize is that many of these diaconal candidates had little to no background in philosophy. When teaching dogmatic theology and attempting, for example, to make distinctions about person and nature in the Most Blessed Trinity, it is very difficult to explain things clearly if the students have had no background in philosophy.

Philosophy gives us categories, definitions, and distinctions and offers us a real framework on which to base our theology. It does not tell us necessarily *what* to think, but more so teaches us *how* to think. And when we study the history of philosophy, we can see the great interchange that exists between faith and culture. One needs only to look to the formulation of the Nicene Creed to see how much we use philosophical terms to express our theological faith. Pope Saint John Paul II begins his encyclical *Fides et Ratio* (On the Relationship between Faith and Reason) with the statement that "faith and reason are like two wings on which the human spirit rises to the contemplation of truth." As such, philosophy and theology, although separate disciplines, work together and are not in opposition.

> *Faith and reason are like two wings on which the*
> *human spirit rises to the contemplation of truth.*
> (Pope Saint John Paul II)

What Philosophy Classes Should I Study if I Want to Be a Theologian?

Well, we have to nuance the question a bit, making the distinction between someone who is studying theology formally and someone who just wants to learn more about his or her faith. In either case, philosophy will certainly help, but for the academic student, the Church has made suggestions as to what classes one should have in philosophy before one begins a serious, academic study of theology.

The United States Conference of Catholic Bishops, in the sixth edition of their *Program of Priestly Formation* — which is based on Pope Saint John Paul II's masterful post-synodal exhortation *Pastores Dabo Vobis* (On the Formation of Priests in the Circumstances of the Present Day)[1] — suggests the following plan of study.

1) History of Philosophy

When we learn what the great thinkers of the past and the present — those with whom we agree and those with whom we must, as people of faith, disagree — have taught, we learn about what humanity is thinking. From ancients such as Plato and Aristotle, we can learn some of the thought that influenced Saint John the Evangelist, the Church Father Saint Augustine, and Saint Thomas Aquinas. Saint Thomas appreciated Aristotle in particular and is said to have "baptized" Aristotle's thought by adapting his ancient, pre-Christian wisdom to the formation of a true Christian philosophy. When we study the thought of the medieval philosophers, including not only Saint Thomas (1225–1274) but John Duns Scotus (1266–1308), William of Ockham (1287–1347), and many others, we can see the roots of our contemporary world's notion of self and reality.

For instance, John Duns Scotus's concept of univocity is believed by some to be the primary factor in the loss of an analogical sense of reality, which in turn can lead to a distortion of an authentically Christian understanding of God. The effects of Scotus's denial of analogy and promotion of univocity and nominalism[2] led to the Enlightenment, which in turn led to modernity, which in turn led to the secular state of postmodernity.[3]

In the history of modern philosophy, René Descartes (1596–1650) is particularly important and fascinating because, unlike great thinkers before him, he separated human thinking from faith. This approach led to the Western concept of individualism, which we encounter in so many ways today. There have been notable Catholic responses to this way of thinking, such as in the philosophy of Christian personalism, as exemplified by the Catholic philosophers Jacques Maritain (1882–1973) and Emmanuel Mounier (1905–1950). Still other Catholic philosophers, such as the Canadian Jesuit Bernard Lonergan (1904–1984), have chosen to engage thinkers such as Immanuel Kant (1724–1804) in dialogue.

2) Logic

One may ask why the study of logic, something many of us associate with Star Trek's Mr. Spock and his fellow Vulcans, helps us in our understanding of the faith of the Church. When I am asked this question, I usually raise my eyebrow à la Leonard Nimoy and mention that there is no real separation between faith and reason — although they are certainly distinct — and that learning how to reason and how to make a coherent argument can only aid in understanding and transmitting the Faith credibly.

3) Epistemology

This is the study of knowledge; it is an examination of how humans think and the kinds of things they can come to know. Epistemology helps us determine what is true and assists us in avoiding what is false. It is vital to understand this topic before studying any form of theology, especially moral or dogmatic theology.

4) Metaphysics

A solid grounding in metaphysics is essential for the creation of a Catholic theological method. As a branch of philosophy, metaphysics is "[t]he study of the ultimate causes and constituents of reality."[4] One can see just how vital a proper understanding of metaphysics is in formulating a doctrine of God.

5) Ethics

"Do good, avoid evil" was a basic axiom of Saint Thomas Aquinas, and the study of ethics teaches us to do precisely this. Ethics is the study of the moral principles that assist the human being to freely determine right and wrong.

6) Natural Theology

This is an essential preparation for the study of theology because it examines the nature of God, his existence, and his attributes.

7) Philosophical Anthropology

At its essence, this is the study of what it means to be a human being. If we can begin to understand the mystery that is humankind, this, in turn, can lead us to a study of what it means to be a human being in light of Christ (which is called theological anthropology and is part of dogmatic theology).

8) Political Philosophy

This field is one that the Vatican's Congregation for Catholic Education is now insisting that students beginning their study of theology have already completed. The essential reason is that the Christian, although not of the world, must be in the world and become an active participant in civic life, bringing his or her Christian faith to enlighten every situation.

Do I Have to Go Back to School for All of This?

Simply put, and to state it again even more emphatically — no. But, if one wants to really engage in some serious Catholic theological study, then at least a familiarity with these topics is essential.[5]

Do I Really Need to Study These Ancient Languages?

Saint Thérèse once commented: "In Heaven only shall we be in possession of the clear truth. On earth, even in matters of Holy Scripture, our vision is dim. It distresses me to see the differences in its translations, and had I been a Priest I would have learned Hebrew, so as to read the Word of God as He deigned to utter it in human speech."

One does not have to be a priest to study the classical and biblical languages. Does one have to know them in order to study theology? Again, I will say that it depends on the level at which you wish to engage in your studies. Yes, the Holy Bible has been translated into many modern languages; however, one is not able to fully understand the nuances and subtleties that exist in the Gospels, for example, without a basic knowledge of New Testament Greek. Likewise, some basic Hebrew will really assist the student of theology in appreciating the Old Testament and its theology. Latin is still the official language of the Church in terms of documents, and knowledge of it is necessary for theological students who want to delve more deeply into liturgical and canonical texts.

The Fonts of Divine Revelation

Once we have our bearings in faith and in philosophy, where should our study of theology take us? Truly Catholic theology begins first and foremost with the deposit of Divine Revelation, expressed first in Sacred Scripture and then in Sacred Tradition. It's important for us to recall that God is the author of the Bible. Through the power of the Holy Spirit, he inspires the human author and so moves him, using the human author's intellect and experience, so that he truthfully expresses and accurately writes down all that God intends and only what God intends.[6]

> *Truly Catholic theology begins first and foremost with the deposit of Divine Revelation, expressed first in Sacred Scripture and then in Sacred Tradition.*

As we know, the Bible is a collection of books consisting of different literary genres. In it, we find history, poetry, songs, and canticles, among other genres. The Bible is divided into two parts, the Old Testament and the New Testament. The Old Testament is made up of the Pentateuch (meaning "five books"), known by the Jewish people as the Law (the *Torah* in Hebrew); the writings of the prophets (the *Nevi'im*); and the Writings (the *Ketuvim*).[7] We as Catholics hold that there are forty-six books in the Old Testament.[8] The New Testament consists of twenty-seven books, including the four Gospels (written by the evangelists Matthew, Mark, Luke, and John), the Acts of the Apostles (written by Saint Luke), the Letters, or Epistles (primarily written by Saint Paul), and the Book of Revelation (attributed to Saint John).

By Sacred Tradition, we mean that through the power of the Holy Spirit, the Church hands down (*traditio*) the lived experience of "all that she herself is, all that she believes" (*Dei Verbum* [Dogmatic Constitution on Divine Revelation] 8). At its essence, Tradition is the "foundational self-revelation of God that was completed with Christ and the New Testament community."[9] *Dei Verbum* 9 tells us clearly: "Sacred Tradition and Sacred Scripture, then, are bound closely together, and communicate one with the other. For both of them, flowing out from the same divine wellspring, come together in some fashion to form one thing, and move towards the same goal."

Beyond these two fonts of Divine Revelation, Sacred Scripture and Sacred Tradition, we as Catholics are blessed to have the Magisterium of the Church. *Dei Verbum* 10 teaches: "The task of giving an authentic interpretation of the Word of God, whether in its written form or in the Tradition, has been entrusted to the living teaching office of the Church alone. Its authority in this matter is exercised in the name of Jesus Christ." In other words, we as Catholics look to the pope and the bishops in union with him to help us understand the single Deposit of Faith that comes from Divine Revelation. Only after these stages should positive theology come into play.

Points to Remember

- Faith in Christ and his Church is essential if one is to be a theologian.
- The student of theology needs to know how to use the tools of other areas of study, such as philosophy, history, and sociology, while never losing sight of the fact that he or she is studying a sacred science in theology.
- The student of theology must have a firm understanding of how to think. This is where the study of philosophy comes into play.
- The Church, although she has no "official" philosophy, recommends, above all else, a firm grounding in the thought of Saint Thomas Aquinas.

- Knowing Latin, Greek, and Hebrew, although not
essential for the study of theology, can really help
the student understand the Bible, the Fathers of the
Church, and other important Church texts.

Suggestions for Further Reading

For further reading concerning topics in this chapter, you might
want to consult the following:

- Pope Saint John Paul II, *Fides et Ratio* (1998)
- Congregation for the Doctrine of the Faith, *Donum
Veritatis* (Instruction on the Ecclesial Vocation of
the Theologian) (1990)
- Pope Leo XIII, *Aeterni Patris* (1879)

3

Why Are There So
Many "Ologies"?

One of the things that can intimidate a person who is beginning his or her study of theology is all of the branches of theology that are out there. As I explained in the previous chapters, theology is ultimately the study of God and the things of God, which one has to do with and in the Church as a person of faith. The study of theology has to rely upon the "skeleton" of a solid philosophy, and it needs to proceed with an examination of Divine Revelation — Sacred Scripture and Sacred Tradition. From there, we study what the Magisterium, the official teaching of the Catholic Church, has to say about an issue. Only after this foundation has been established does positive theology enter into the picture. In the next chapter, I'll offer more detail on the proper use of philosophy within theology, along with what we mean as Catholics when we speak of interpreting Sacred Scripture and Sacred Tradition. I will also discuss how the *Catechism of the Catholic Church* and the documents of the Second Vatican Council can be used in the beginnings of Catholic theological study.

Before we get into that further detail, however, let's wrap our minds around the various branches of theology. When one goes to a Catholic bookstore and sees all of the theology books, it can be more than a bit confusing! The proliferation of "ologies" out there can be really intimidating. Christology, eschatology, ecclesiology, pneumatology — what does it all mean? Like any academic field, theology has its own set of technical phrases. Many of these phrases come from Latin and Greek roots. Eschatology is the study of the four last things — death, Judgment, heaven, and hell.[1] We can see the Greek word *eschatos*, meaning "last," in this word. Pneumatology has as its root the Greek word *pneuma*, meaning "spirit"; hence, pneumatology is the study of the Holy Spirit. The study of the Church is called ecclesiology, which has its basis in the Greek word *ekklesia*, meaning "church."[2]

A caveat on overspecialization: As we will see later in this text, some theologians develop the bad habit of becoming so specialized in one branch of theology that they lose sight of the big picture. If asked in what field of theology he would consider himself to be a master, Saint Thomas Aquinas, for all his work in what we would consider dogmatic or moral theology, would probably have answered, "Scripture." He was a master of *Sacra Doctrina* (Sacred Doctrine).[3]

Sacra Doctrina

In his greatest work, the *Summa Theologiae*, Saint Thomas Aquinas states: "It is therefore necessary that besides philosophical science there should be a sacred science learned through revelation."[4] In stating this, he's saying that this sacred science — what the Church also refers to as *Sacra Doctrina*, or Sacred Doctrine — is distinct from the philosophical disciplines, as important as they are (and it is necessary for us to recall that, for Saint Thomas, the term "philosophical" as used here encompasses all of human learning). *Sacra Doctrina* is different from all the other types of learning because of its source: God's Revelation.

It's important at this point to state that Saint Thomas was not holding *Sacra Doctrina* to a less rigorous standard than human knowledge. In fact, *Sacra Doctrina* has to be even more rigorous because, although it is like some branches of human knowledge, in that it involves an explanation of a text, the text on which *Sacra Doctrina* bases itself is Sacred Scripture, which is the divinely revealed Word of God. As one of my students once observed, *Sacra Doctrina* is "the systematic unpacking of the inspired texts of Scripture."

> **Sacra Doctrina** *begins with the Divine. It is precisely this divine light, the light of Divine Revelation, that illuminates each and every bit of this science. It is for this reason that theology is the "queen of all the sciences" and that "philosophy is the handmaiden to theology."*

There is a unity in *Sacra Doctrina* because its source is the One who is in himself Truth, Goodness, Beauty, and Unity. It does not start with human principles and gradually work its way up to the Divine; rather, *Sacra Doctrina* begins with the Divine. It is precisely this divine light, the light of Divine Revelation, that illuminates each and every bit of this science. It is for this reason that theology is the "queen of all the sciences" and "philosophy is the handmaiden to theology."

The Breakdown of Theology into Specializations

The study of theology was basically approached as a unified whole until, in the university systems, and for various historical, philosophical, and cultural reasons, theology was broken down into fields of specialization. As I mentioned, this is not a bad thing in and of itself — as long as we do not lose the essential unity of the faith. When I did my own licentiate and doctoral degrees in theology, my specialization was in a field called fundamental theology, which I will describe for you shortly. However, for most of my priesthood I have taught Church history, moral theology, New Testament, and dogmatic theology. Why? Because that is what was needed in the programs and schools in which I was teaching. The lesson to be learned is simple: The theologian can specialize in any field he or she wants but has to be ready to know and express more than just his or her specialization.

All of these theological subjects can seem so refined and obscure. When one studies one field or one aspect of theology (or, as happens in advanced studies, one might focus on a single thinker within a field of theology — I studied the American twentieth-century theologian John Courtney Murray), one can become very familiar with one line of thought while not knowing all that much about other areas. For instance, when I have an in-depth question about a situation involving moral theology, because I spent my own advanced studies in fundamental and historical theology, I go and ask someone who has specialized in moral theology. This is natural and good. We need specialists! But in order to become a really qualified specialist in an area, we must have a basic understanding of theology as a whole. It would do someone who is beginning theological studies no good to start with a highly complex theological treatise. It's important to learn the basics first, get the fundamentals down; then — and only then — can one specialize.

So what are the fields within theology? Please keep in mind that the approach I outline below is only one way to divide the fields. There are many other ways to do so, depending on where you study.

1) Fundamental Theology
This is a branch of theology that studies the transmission of Di-

vine Revelation through Sacred Scripture and Sacred Tradition, as well as how the Magisterium of the Church interprets them. It also speaks about the credibility of Divine Revelation, which is the field of apologetics. Fundamental theology is the area where theology is in dialogue with culture, science, and philosophy. As one can imagine, it is an essential field for the promotion of the New Evangelization. Faith, belief and unbelief, atheism, agnosticism, and secular humanism are all considered in the area of fundamental theology. One might say that fundamental theology is the "why" of theology. An important Vatican II document that can help us understand fundamental theology is *Dei Verbum*. The *Catechism of the Catholic Church*, part one, section one, chapters one to three, cover much of the material studied in fundamental theology.

2) Dogmatic Theology

This is the field that is, in many ways, the "what" of theology. It deals with the doctrine of the Faith. It studies God, both as One and as the Most Blessed Trinity. It discusses Christology (who Jesus is) as well as soteriology (how Jesus is Savior). It includes pneumatology (the study of the Holy Spirit). It studies the Church and who we are as members of the Church (for which Vatican II's *Lumen Gentium* [Dogmatic Constitution on the Church] is a great aid to our understanding), as well as the manner in which the Church relates to and engages with the world (for which Vatican II's *Gaudium et Spes* [Pastoral Constitution on the Church in the Modern World] offers a great explanation). Dogma covers Mariology (the study of the Blessed Mother) and grace (God's life within us). In addition, theological anthropology (the study of who man is in light of Christ) is part of dogmatic theology, as are protology (the study of creation) and eschatology (the study of the four last things — death, Judgment, heaven, and hell). Finally, dogmatic theology studies the sacraments of the Church. In the

Catechism of the Catholic Church, part one, section two, chapters one to three, and part two, sections one and two, describe much of the content of dogmatic theology.

3) Moral Theology

By delving into the roots of Sacred Scripture, Sacred Tradition, the Magisterium, and positive theology, the study of moral theology equips a student to know what the Church teaches and how it can be practically applied to concrete situations. I suggest that someone seeking a basic overview of the Church's moral theology could turn to the *Catechism of the Catholic Church*, part three: Life in Christ, section one: Man's Vocation: Life in the Spirit. Another excellent resource is Saint John Paul II's 1993 encyclical *Veritatis Splendor* (The Splendor of Truth).

4) Historical Theology

George Santayana famously wrote: "Those who cannot remember the past are condemned to repeat it." Through a firm grasp of our Church's history, we can learn where we've been and understand where we should be headed. This study can also provide us serenity in the midst of controversies that surround the Church, both the major ones and the minor ones, reminding us that Christ is the Lord of history and that he is guiding the Church through time. It can also free us from being slaves to the present moment, rushing into this, or attaching ourselves to that. Knowing the Church's history can give us the perspective we need to make sound decisions in the light of Christ.

In this category, I not only include Church history proper, but also the history of theology, which is a vital subject in which we learn how a theological concept grows and changes through the Church and her theologians. The study of the Fathers of the Church (patrology) and their writings and theology (patristic theology) is also part of this specialization.

5) Biblical Theology

The study of the Bible was described by Vatican II as the "soul of theology" (*Dei Verbum* 24), and indeed it is. The study of God's word in Sacred Scripture leads us to a discovery of God's Word made flesh in Jesus Christ. Sometimes when we think of studying the Bible, we assume we need to have mastered biblical Greek and Hebrew and to have complex exegetical, historical, and archeological details at our fingertips. Although a formal study of biblical theology is enriching, it is best for someone just starting theological study to simply prayerfully read the Bible itself. Read it as a narrative; get to know the story of both the Old and the New Testaments. Doing this makes it apparent just how much theology is in every inspired word of Sacred Scripture. Pope Benedict XVI's 2010 post-synodal apostolic exhortation *Verbum Domini* (On the Word of God in the Life and Mission of the Church) and Vatican II's *Dei Verbum* are helpful texts in understanding how the Church interprets Sacred Scripture.

The study of God's word in Sacred Scripture leads us to a discovery of God's Word made flesh in Jesus Christ.

6) Spiritual Theology

Spiritual theology is the study of the history of spirituality in the Catholic tradition, examining some of the great thinkers and "pray-ers" of the Church. This includes the Fathers and Doctors of the Church, as well as the great Catholic spiritual masters. Spiritual theology also involves a study of the specific states of the Christian life and a practical "how-to" for prayer and spiritual direction. A great book for beginning the study of Christian spirituality is Jordan Aumann, OP's *Christian Spirituality in the Catholic Tradition* (Ignatius, 1985).

7) Liturgical Theology

This is the field of theology that exemplifies the motto *"lex orandi, lex credendi"* ("the law of prayer is the law of belief"). The celebration of the Sacred Liturgy is that privileged place that deepens and expresses most fully the Faith we profess. Liturgical theology is more than just knowing the rubrics, more than just understanding the words and actions during a liturgy. It involves exploring the history, theology, and experience of the Church — all of which are present in the celebration of the Liturgy of the Hours and the Holy Mass. Liturgical study is an important branch of theology, which is why great thinkers such as Romano Guardini and Joseph Ratzinger spent so much time writing and teaching about this field. It touches and makes concrete in celebration our morals and dogma.

8) Pastoral Theology

Now, this field is going to take a little bit longer to explain. The *Catholic Encyclopedia* tells us, "Pastoral theology is the science of the care of souls." Pastoral theology is best illustrated by our Lord Jesus, the Master Teacher. In the Gospel of John, chapter 4, Jesus meets the woman at the well. This encounter of Christ with the Samaritan woman, who is simply looking for some water, is a supreme example of what Pope Francis calls "accompaniment." In his apostolic exhortation *Evangelii Gaudium*, the pope describes accompaniment as an art, a skill. He states: "The Church will have to initiate everyone — priests, religious and laity — into this 'art of accompaniment' which teaches us to remove our sandals before the sacred ground of the other (cf. Ex 3:5)" (169).

Jesus, in the Gospel, meets the woman where she is: literally, at the well. She is there simply looking to fetch a pail of water. And the Lord Jesus — he who is all truth — meets her there and leads her gently, patiently, to truth. Notice that it is the Lord himself who initiates conversation with her. He, a devout Jew, deigns to speak to a Samaritan — one who is unclean by birth, a member of a sect of Judaism that had broken far away from the mainstream religion and intermarried with foreigners. On top of that, Jesus is speaking to a woman. In those days, no man would speak in public to a strange woman, if both he and she were to be considered respectable.

Jesus asks her for some water. And this stops her in her tracks. He asks her to go out of herself, if only for a moment, and to enter into service. This is why true conversions of faith happen when we engage people in service projects, in helping the poor, for instance. In serving others we go from the natural level — from a natural desire to help others — to the supernatural level of beginning to recognize Christ in the midst of the people we are serving. Think of all the vocations to priesthood and religious life that begin with service projects in the parish.

The Lord Jesus gradually engages this woman, meeting her where she is, and through dialogue, patience, charity, and humility, he brings her to where she must be — namely, to friendship with him. This is the art of accompaniment of which the pope speaks: "Genuine spiritual accompaniment always begins and flourishes in the context of service to the mission of evangelization" (*EG* 173). The pope explains further: "Spiritual accompaniment must lead others ever closer to God. … To accompany them would be counterproductive if it became a sort of therapy supporting their self-absorption and ceased to be a pilgrimage with Christ to the Father" (*EG* 170).

Although this accompaniment is not about watering down the truth, the Lord Jesus, who knows the hearts of all, does not begin his conversation with this woman with a laundry list of her sins. But he helps her understand her situation in life, her many sins. He helps her comprehend for the first time that she is truly thirsting for the living water that only the Lord Jesus, who is life and truth, can give. In his dialogue with her, the Lord shows us the art of accompaniment. Pope Francis writes: "Listening, in communication, is an openness of heart which makes possible that closeness without which genuine spiritual encounter cannot occur" (*EG* 171).

It's the job of priests and those involved in apostolic service to know what the Church teaches and to present it clearly. We have to model the truth of the Faith by living it out daily. We can't water down the truth, especially about marriage, life issues (for nothing is more essential than the sanctity of life), the integrity of the sacraments (especially the Holy Eucharist), and issues of sexuality and gender. We have to know what the Church teaches and to be able to communicate it clearly and concisely.

> **We have to know what the Church teaches and to be able to communicate it clearly and concisely. But communication is a two-way street.**

But communication is a two-way street — a true dialogue. As Pope Francis writes: "Dialogue is born from a respectful attitude toward the other person, from a conviction that the other person has something good to say. It supposes that we can make room in our heart for their point of view, their opinion and their proposals. Dialogue entails a warm reception and not a preemptive condemnation. To dialogue, one must know how to lower the defenses, to open the doors of one's home and to offer warmth."[5]

True dialogue doesn't mean smiling and listening, nodding along, and giving tacit approval. Nor does it mean lecturing another person. Jesus engages in dialogue, but he is pretty direct when it comes to the reality of the presence of sin in the woman's life. And yet he who is mercy walks with her. What does this mean?

It means that pastoral theology requires beginning on the natural level — and then moving to the supernatural level. Through the Spirit working in our midst, we go deeper and deeper to engage with another person, not just on the level of emotions, and not just on the level of the intellect, but on the level of the soul.

The Gospel of the woman at the well is a masterpiece of the art of accompaniment. The Lord Jesus meets her where she is and exposes her gradually to the truth without watering it down. And then, once she sees the truth and begins to embrace it, what does she do? She goes and brings others to see this man, the Lord Jesus, who knows everything about her. This art of accompaniment is a fine and necessary tool in the work of evangelization, and it is the supreme exemplification of the science of pastoral theology.

This All Seems like Drinking from a Firehose ... It's a Lot!

Given all of this rich theology within the Church, how does one even begin to get the basics down? Just recall what I mentioned already: Have faith in Christ and in his Church. Yearn to learn all about someone whom you love and who loves you, someone with whom you have a deep, true, intimate relationship in and through his Bride, the Church. Start with Divine Revelation as expressed in and through its fonts of Sacred Scripture and Sacred Tradition. Get to understand the story of the Bible as a narrative first, before you study any exegetical method. Get to know the contents of the *Catechism of the Catholic Church*, which is a great gift to the Church from Pope Saint John Paul II. Come to an understanding, to the extent that you can, of some basic philosophical principles. Above all, have faith, and that faith will lead you to a desire for understanding. From here, we can develop a basic theological method.

Points to Remember

- Theology is a science whose object — God — makes it distinct.

- Philosophy is the handmaiden to the "queen," theology.
- Although theology has become specialized, the good theologian should attempt to see the unity in all theology rather than the disunity.

Suggestions for Further Reading

For further reading concerning topics in this chapter, you might want to consult the following:

- Gerald O'Collins, SJ, and Edward G. Farrugia, SJ, eds., *A Concise Dictionary of Theology*, rev. ed. (Mahwah, NJ/New York: Paulist, 2000).
- James T. Bretzke, SJ, *Consecrated Phrases: A Latin Theological Dictionary; Latin Expressions Commonly Found in Theological Writings*, 3rd ed. (Collegeville, MN: Michael Glazier, 2013).

4

How Do I Form a Theological Method?

P art of my job as academic dean of a seminary that sends students out to various universities and other academic institutes is to keep track not only of where my seminarians are studying, but also of what they are studying and the approach in how it is taught. For our "first cycle" (that is, the first three years of major seminary, in which a seminarian studies for his bachelor's in sacred theology), each of our students attends one of three pontifical universities, all of which are top-notch and all of which are teaching, more or less, the same material. Although the pontifical universities teach similar material, they generally do so using different theological methods. This doesn't mean that they are in opposition to each other or that they are teaching things contrary to each other. It only means that they have different ways of approaching theology.

What Is Theological Method? Why Is It Needed?

Why should a topic as personal as theology, which involves the study of God and the things of God, have a particular methodology imposed on it? C. S. Lewis responds to this question by emphasizing how necessary it is to clarify terminology, set limitations regarding what will be studied, and outline a clear, concise roadmap before engaging in any level of serious study. He writes:

> The first qualification for judging any piece of workmanship from a corkscrew to a cathedral is to know what it is — what it was intended to do and how it is meant to be used. After that has been discovered the temperance reformer may decide that the corkscrew was made for a bad purpose, and the communist may think the same about the cathedral. But such questions come later. The first thing is to understand the object before you: as long as you think the corkscrew was meant for opening tins or the cathedral for entertaining tourists you can say nothing to the purpose about them.[1]

In other words, one needs to understand the approach, or the method, before one can understand the theology that is being examined. One needs to understand the theological method employed by a particular theologian before one can grasp the theology that he or she is mining from the fonts of Revelation (namely, Sacred Scripture and Sacred Tradition). J. J. Mueller writes: "Because method never sits apart from the theologian who wields it or from the content of theology that is generated, the task is a challenging one."[2]

> **One needs to understand the approach, or the method, before one can understand the theology that is being examined.**

In addition to the difficulty of explaining the need for theological method in general, there is also the difficulty of explaining its pastoral significance. Most involved in Christian ministry spend very little conscious time pondering issues of theological method; yet it really is of the utmost importance in the Christian endeavor. What manner, what approach, should one bring to the transmission of the Christian faith? Ross A. Shecterle writes: "There can be no divine revelation without some form of human mediation. To inquire into the character of revelation is to inquire into the fashion in which we come to know it. The category of mediation is essential to the discussion of revelation."[3] You see, God is the author of Divine Revelation. He reveals himself to us through divinely inspired Sacred Scripture and Sacred Tradition. However, we, as limited human beings, must still interpret that Divine Revelation and, further, communicate this divine self-communication to the world.

Two Different Approaches to a Theological Method

There are far more than just two types of theological method — but for our purpose here, to show how theology can be tackled in various ways, I would like to present two different approaches to theology, both of which have stood the test of time. One approach is called positive theology, and the other is called Scholastic theology. Each relies on God's Revelation and the human minds that consider that Revelation, but they take slightly different paths to theology.

Positive Theology

This is the method of approaching theology in which I was trained. It examines the fonts of Divine Revelation — the inspired Word of God found in Sacred Scripture and the unchanging, Sacred Tradition of the Church. Further on in this line of study, because the theologian does not exist in a vacuum, he examines what the Church's Magisterium has taught about a particular question, as well as what other branches of (nontheological) learning might contribute to the conversation. This is an approach that is clearly used in the Second Vatican Council's Dogmatic Constitution on Divine Revelation, and it is one that many theologians (Joseph Ratzinger, for instance) have used to produce theological works.

I will try to demonstrate what it might look like for us to use this method concerning a theological question. I recognize there isn't room to delve deeply into Sacred Scripture and Sacred Tradition or the Magisterium in a few paragraphs. But, let's briefly approach a specific question involving Mariology — What does it mean for the Blessed Virgin Mary to be perpetually virgin before, during, and after childbirth? — using positive theology.

The method used in positive theology would have us first turn to Sacred Scripture. In the Old Testament, the prophet Isaiah tells us: "Therefore the Lord himself will give you a sign. Behold, a virgin shall conceive and bear a son, and shall call his name Immanuel" (Is 7:14). Then, turning to the New Testament, we read the following:

> In the sixth month the angel Gabriel was sent from God to a city of Galilee named Nazareth, to a virgin betrothed to a man whose name was Joseph, of the house of David; and the virgin's name was Mary. And he came to her and said, "Hail, full of grace, the Lord is with you!" But she was greatly troubled at the saying, and considered in her mind what sort of greeting this might be. And the angel said to her, "Do not be afraid, Mary, for you have found favor with God. And behold, you will conceive in your womb and bear a son, and you shall call his name Jesus." (Luke 1:26–31)

We can then turn to Sacred Tradition and find the following from the great Father of the Church Saint Ignatius of Antioch (c.

35–108): "You are firmly convinced about our Lord, who is truly of the race of David according to the flesh, Son of God according to the will and power of God, truly born of a virgin, ... he was truly nailed to a tree for us in his flesh under Pontius Pilate ... he truly suffered, as he is also truly risen."[4]

From this point, we can next look to the Magisterium of the Church for guidance on the question. *Lumen Gentium* from Vatican II states:

> By reason of the gift and role of divine maternity, by which she is united with her Son, the Redeemer, and with His singular graces and functions, the Blessed Virgin is also intimately united with the Church. As St. Ambrose taught, the Mother of God is a type of the Church in the order of faith, charity and perfect union with Christ. For in the mystery of the Church, which is itself rightly called mother and virgin, the Blessed Virgin stands out in eminent and singular fashion as exemplar both of virgin and mother. By her belief and obedience, not knowing man but overshadowed by the Holy Spirit, as the new Eve she brought forth on earth the very Son of the Father, showing an undefiled faith, not in the word of the ancient serpent, but in that of God's messenger. The Son whom she brought forth is He whom God placed as the first-born among many brethren, namely the faithful, in whose birth and education she cooperates with a maternal love.[5]

Does this method seem familiar to you? It might if you have read the *Catechism of the Catholic Church*! This is pretty much a simplified version of what is found in paragraphs 495–507 of the *Catechism*. Taking this method further, one would then examine what other theologians throughout the ages, such as Saint Bernard, Saint Thomas Aquinas, Joseph Ratzinger, and Hans Urs von Balthasar, have written concerning this topic.[6]

Scholastic Theology

One can contrast positive theology with Scholastic theology, but I would caution against placing them in opposition to each other. Scholastic theology can be seen as an aid to positive theology and vice versa. Edward Gratsch describes Scholastic theology as "speculative" theology and states: "Scholastic theology examines the truths of revelation in order to explain, develop, and systematize them."[7] The perfect example of Scholastic theology is Saint Thomas Aquinas's masterpiece, the *Summa Theologiae*. Originally intended to be a summary, a synthesis for beginners, it has become perhaps the single most influential tome in the history of theology.

> **The perfect example of Scholastic theology is Saint Thomas Aquinas's masterpiece, the Summa Theologiae ... perhaps the single most influential tome in the history of theology.**

One of the most important aspects of Scholastic theology, as exemplified in the *Summa*, is that it presents the truths of the Faith in an orderly fashion. The first part of the *Summa* is all about God and his creation; the next part is on human happiness; following that is the part on the divine life in humankind; and the last part is on Christ and how we experience him in the sacraments of the Church. It's very easy to come up with a curriculum for theological study when we follow the set-up given in the *Summa Theologiae*.

One of the great things about the *Summa* is that Saint Thomas has already considered the objections that one could make to his arguments. Each question he poses comes with objections, an authority quoted to rebut these objections (*sed contra*), followed by Saint Thomas's response (*respondeo*) to the question and finally his replies to the objections — all of which aim to present the question in a holistic manner.

Let's examine the same theological question regarding Mary from the perspective of Saint Thomas Aquinas's masterpiece. In the *Summa*'s third part, question 28, the Angelic Doctor examines the concept of the perpetual virginity of the Blessed Virgin Mary. Saint Thomas studies this question in four articles, each building on the next. Article 1 asks the question: "Whether the Mother of God was a virgin in conceiving Christ?" Article 2 asks: "Whether Christ's Mother was a virgin in His Birth?" Article 3 asks: "Whether Christ's Mother remained a virgin after His birth?" and Article 4 goes further to inquire: "Whether the Mother of God took a vow of virginity?"

Ever the Master of *Sacra Doctrina*, Saint Thomas draws on the sources of Divine Revelation to answer each of his questions. Let's look to see how he uses the Bible and Tradition. In this third article — "Whether Christ's Mother remained a virgin after His birth?" — he anticipates six opposing arguments. This is the first:

> **Objection 1.** It would seem that Christ's Mother did not remain a virgin after His Birth. For it is written (Matthew 1:18): "Before Joseph and Mary came together, she was found with child of the Holy Ghost." Now the Evangelist would not have said this — "before they came together" — unless he were certain of their subsequent coming together; for no one says of one who does not eventually dine "before he dines" (cf. Jerome, Contra Helvid.). It seems, therefore, that the Blessed Virgin subsequently had intercourse with Joseph; and consequently that she did not remain a virgin after (Christ's) Birth.

After laying out a series of arguments, each relying upon sources in Divine Revelation, demonstrating that the Blessed Mother having remained a virgin after Christ's birth is reasonable, Saint Thomas goes further. One by one, he answers the objections, still armed with Sacred Scripture and Sacred Tradition. For instance, in his response to objection 1 above, he writes:

> **Reply to Objection 1.** As Jerome says (Contra Helvid. i): "Although this particle 'before' often indicates a subsequent event, yet we must observe that it not infrequently points merely to some thing previously in the mind: nor is there need that what was in the mind take place eventually, since something may occur to prevent its happening. Thus if a man say: 'Before I dined in the port, I set sail,' we do not understand him to have dined in port after he set sail: but that his mind was set on dining in port." In like manner the evangelist says: "Before they came together" Mary "was found with child, of the Holy Ghost," not that they came together afterwards: but that, when it seemed that they would come together, this was forestalled through her conceiving by the Holy Ghost, the result being that afterwards they did not come together.

What Do Positive Theology and Scholastic Theology Have in Common?

Scholastic theology and positive theology have many things in common, but for the sake of this simple, introductory text, the most obvious thing they share is their use of the fonts of Divine Revelation, namely Sacred Scripture and Sacred Tradition. In the next chapter, we will examine first how to use Sacred Scripture for theology; following that, we will consider what Sacred Tradition is and isn't.

Points to Remember

- There are several different methods one could use in studying a theological question.
- Positive theology examines the fonts of Divine Revelation — the inspired Word of God found in the Sacred Scriptures and the unchanging Sacred Tradition of the Church — to come to know what God has revealed about himself.
- Scholastic theology examines the truths of Revelation in order to explain, develop, and systematize them.
- Although Scholastic theology and positive theology approach theology in different manners, they both rely on the fonts of Divine Revelation (Sacred Scripture and Sacred Tradition).

Suggestions for Further Reading

For further reading concerning topics in this chapter, you might want to consult the following:

- Jared Wicks, *Introduction to Theological Method* (Casale Monferrato: Piemme, 1994).
- Aidan Nichols, OP, *The Shape of Catholic Theology: An Introduction to Its Sources, Principles, and History* (Edinburgh: T&T Clarke, 1991).
- Ulrich G. Leinsle, *Introduction to Scholastic Theology*, trans. Michael J. Miller (Washington, DC: Catholic University of America Press, 2011).

5

How Do I Use the "Tools" of Theology — Sacred Scripture and Sacred Tradition? Some Personal Examples

The "tools" of theological method are the fonts of Divine Revelation — Sacred Scripture and Sacred Tradition. God desires to enter into a relationship with mankind. The *Catechism* teaches us:

> By natural reason man can know God with certainty, on the basis of his works. But there is another order of knowledge, which man cannot possibly arrive at by his own powers: the order of divine Revelation. Through an utterly free decision, God has revealed himself and given himself to man. This he does by revealing the mystery, his plan of loving goodness, formed from all eternity in Christ, for the benefit of all men. God has fully revealed

this plan by sending us his beloved Son, our Lord Jesus Christ, and the Holy Spirit. (50)

And further, in a series of direct quotes from the Second Vatican Council's *Dei Verbum*, the *Catechism* states:

"Sacred Tradition and Sacred Scripture, then, are bound closely together, and communicate one with the other. For both of them, flowing out from the same divine well-spring, come together in some fashion to form one thing, and move towards the same goal." Each of them makes present and fruitful in the Church the mystery of Christ, who promised to remain with his own "always, to the close of the age."

"*Sacred Scripture* is the speech of God as it is put down in writing under the breath of the Holy Spirit."

"And [Holy] *Tradition* transmits in its entirety the Word of God which has been entrusted to the apostles by Christ the Lord and the Holy Spirit. It transmits it to the successors of the apostles so that, enlightened by the Spirit of truth, they may faithfully preserve, expound and spread it abroad by their preaching."

As a result the Church, to whom the transmission and interpretation of Revelation is entrusted, "does not derive her certainty about all revealed truths from the holy Scriptures alone. Both Scripture and Tradition must be accepted and honored with equal sentiments of devotion and reverence." (80–82)

In the following pages I offer some personal reflections on the four Gospels and the Fathers of the Church. It is my hope that they might serve as examples of how to put the "tools" of theology to work in our spiritual and pastoral lives.

The Call of Matthew and Double Discernment

There is a certain joy to living in Rome. Yes, I do spend some of my days in absolute frustration over my host country of Italy. Italians are very different from most Americans. They move at a slower pace in many ways. They tend to appreciate the finer things in life, and they take their time in doing things that would go much more quickly in the United States. I had some visitors to Rome recently, and one of them wanted to get a haircut. I brought him to the local barber, and what would most likely have been a ten-minute haircut at home in the United States became a forty-minute work of art. I can tell you that this gentleman and his wife were amazed at the barber's care, his skill, and the end result. But it took so long! Add to this the experience of being on a city bus in Rome, and you might understand the frustration that I feel sometimes.

But I am blessed to live in a place where our local parish is Saint Peter's Basilica, where our local bishop is the pope, and where we need not go to a museum to see famous works of art but merely to a nearby church. Yes, for the vast majority of the seminarians whom I teach, one such church that houses a famous piece of art by Caravaggio is on the way to their universities.

Caravaggio's *The Calling of Saint Matthew*, painted for the Contarelli Chapel in the Church of San Luigi dei Francesi, is the work that most art scholars believe made his reputation as an artist. Coming out of the darkness on the right-hand side of the painting is Our Lord with Saint Peter, his vicar. Interestingly, both Our Lord and Saint Peter are gesturing toward Matthew, who could be any one of the five males gathered at the table, from the youngest boy to the old man.

If you examine the picture, you will see that the Lord Jesus extends his hand in a manner remarkably similar to the way God the Father extends his to Adam in Michelangelo's earlier Sistine Chapel painting. As the Lord makes this gesture, so too, in his shadow, does Saint Peter, albeit weakly: Saint Peter imitates the Lord's gesture to the men. This painting of the famous Gospel scene can serve to illustrate what it means to have a priestly vocation.

It is the Lord Jesus who calls men to his service in priestly ministry. It is the Lord Jesus — and he alone — who is the source and summit of the call to the priesthood, and all priests stand in response to his call. However, that call of the Lord Jesus is mediated to men through Saint Peter and through the Church.

It is not enough for someone who feels called to serve the Lord as his priest to attend a Rite of Ordination, say for himself "*Adsum*" ("I am present"), and get in line to have hands laid on him by a bishop. Rather, he needs to have that individual call of the Lord to which he is responding affirmed by the Church, which can only come about through years of priestly formation. It is a double discernment, if you will — the seminarian discerning his call to the priesthood, and the Church, in and through the process of formation, discerning along with him. This is why seminary formation takes years and years. There are many agents of formation who discern alongside a seminarian — the vocation director, the formation staff, the rector, and, ultimately, the bishop. The formation of a priest is not merely a matter of gaining pastoral skills and experience. It's not just about acquiring academic knowledge. This is why the priests who serve in seminary formation must understand their roles as spiritual fathers to the seminarians, who are precious gifts that the Lord has entrusted to the formators.

As we contemplate Caravaggio's painting of the call of Matthew — one who heard the call of the Lord and responded — we can pray for a true understanding of the "double discernment" that is necessary in every priestly vocation. The discernment of the candidate is represented by Matthew, and the discernment of the agents of formation is represented by Saint Peter, who extends his weak hand in imitation of the one who makes it strong — the Lord Jesus Christ. Pray for your seminarians that they might be holy and just men who have discerned their calls wisely and well through the process of priestly formation in the Church.

Learning from Mark's Gospel

We now turn to Mark's Gospel. Mark is the most bare-bones of the Gospels. I've been told one could successfully read this Gospel in Greek with an understanding of about eighty to one hundred Greek words. The Gospel of Mark is written for Gentiles — that is, non-Jewish Christians; in many ways, it is the exact opposite of Matthew's Gospel, which is written for Jewish Christians. While Matthew's Gospel has a great many little references (and some not so little) to the Old Testament, Mark's Gospel is a beginner's manual, an introduction on a basic level to who Jesus is and what Jesus is all about!

Mark's Gospel is clean, clear, and direct. Written around the year A.D. 70, it leaves out a great deal of the information found in the other Gospels. There's no infancy narrative at all. It begins, rather bluntly, with "The beginning of the gospel of Jesus Christ, the Son of God." Mark's Gospel is an almost perfect example of what we call the *kerygma* (proclamation) — it succinctly covers what we used to acclaim in the old English translation of the Mystery of Faith at Mass — "Christ has died, Christ is risen, Christ will come again."

For all its simplicity, Mark's Gospel is much more complex than it may first appear. There are always two levels of action going on in the Gospel. There is the natural level — the events that the Lord finds himself taking part in — and there is the supernatural level. The in-breaking of supernatural grace on the natural level is apparent in Jesus' words and actions (see *Dei Verbum* 2) as he reveals the Kingdom of God — which, as we know, is not simply a place or a concept but rather Jesus himself. He himself is the Kingdom; he is the preacher and the preached, the teacher and that which is taught, the messenger and the message.

> *There are always two levels of action going on in the Gospel. There is the natural level — the events that the Lord finds himself taking part in — and there is the supernatural level.*

In each of Jesus' healings (for example, in Mark 1–3), which take place on the natural level, the supernatural world gets all stirred up, too. Even the demons recognize who Christ is, long before most of the humans do. Jesus prevents the demons from revealing who he is, because it is not yet his time (Mk 3:11).

As we try to live our lives as Christians, there are three things that we can learn from Mark's Gospel: presence, prayer, and patience. First, presence: In one section of Mark's Gospel (Mk 1:29–31), Jesus just shows up at Peter's house. Like a good doctor, this Divine Physician makes a sick call. So much of our lives is spent merely being present to others, even when it may not be the most efficient thing to do. Those in religious life living in community demonstrate the importance of presence time and again. This is one of the great gifts of religious life. Being present in community energizes the sister or brother to then go out and give more of himself or herself away, graciously, in Christ. This is also true in our parishes; we are energized by the presence of our brothers and sisters in the local Church community. Coming together as a parish family for prayer, study, and recreation, we are then able to go out to the world and be the presence of Christ to others.

Second, prayer: Jesus prays (Mk 1:35–39)! He recharges his battery with prayer, with going away to a deserted place. In our lives of commitment to daily prayer (for priests and consecrated, especially in the Liturgy of the Hours), we are blessed to pray for the sanctification not only of ourselves but of the whole world.

We go away to a deserted place when we take the time for the Divine Office or other daily prayer. This *exitus* (departure) into prayer allows us to make a *reditus* (return) to the world in service.

Third, patience: Mark's Gospel tells of the messianic secret, the fact that only God can reveal who Jesus is, and that it can only be revealed in God's time (see Mk 1:40–45). For us who are ordained or in religious life, this sort of patience and timing is illustrated in our obedience to our superiors. I may think the time is right for me to do this or that — much as if Jesus had followed his own will, he could have just done everything right away — but ultimately, I follow the will of the Father, as revealed through my superior. In my case, as a diocesan priest, this requires a tremendous act of faith in God and in the movements of the Holy Spirit in the life of my bishop. For married persons, patience is found in openness to the will and needs of one's spouse and family. For all Catholics, it is an openness and attentiveness to the will of God as revealed in prayer, study, and a properly formed Catholic conscience.

Presence, prayer, and patience: Mark's Gospel offers us all that. Not bad for the simplest and shortest of the Gospels!

On the Joys of Saint Luke's Gospel

I remember well the joy of learning about the four evangelists for the first time. I was a boy in Catholic school in Brooklyn and, from attending Mass, knew that there were different names that were said when the priest at Mass proclaimed "A reading from the Holy Gospel according to … " In second grade, we learned the names of the four Gospel writers: Matthew, Mark, Luke, and John and what their symbols were (I still recall thinking that the name "Mark" sounded like a lion's roar and that "Luke" sounded like an ox's low). As I recall, it wasn't until later on in grade school that we were given more details about each of the Gospels (and what a joy it was to get a full Bible, not just a children's Bible, for

the first time at my Confirmation in 1985; in fact, I still have it —
a copy of the Jerusalem Bible). It wasn't until high school that we
began delving into what each evangelist was up to in his Gospel.

It was quite an experience, learning all about the Gospels in
sophomore religion class in 1987–1988. The priest who taught
us used a fine book titled *In the Midst Stands Jesus: A Pastoral Introduction to the New Testament* by Monsignor Josiah G.
Chatham (St. Pauls/Alba House, 1972). It was through this high
school class, and through this text, that I really began to love what
I would learn later was biblical theology and Christology. If you
ever come across a copy of Monsignor Chatham's book, please
grab it! It is a blessing.

Saint Luke gives us the Gospel of the history of Jesus, the Gospel with all the details.

Saint Luke gives us the Gospel of the history of Jesus, the Gospel
with all the details. I have to admit that I love Luke's Gospel, and I
get very happy when the time comes around for its proclamation
at Mass every third year. In this Gospel, our Lord Jesus is not
quite the stark figure of simplicity found in the extended Passion
narrative that is Mark's Gospel, nor is he the rich, rabbinical Jesus
of Matthew's Gospel. No, this is a Jesus who is for everybody. This
is a Jesus whom the Christians have had time to reflect upon, and
this portrayal of Jesus is theologically much more sophisticated
than that of Saint Mark. This is a Jesus who is a universal savior,
who wills that all be saved and none be lost.

The Gospel of Luke (along with its "sequel," if you will, the
Acts of the Apostles) is addressed to a certain "Theophilus,"
which means "friend of God." So this Gospel is addressed to you
and to me — to those of us who want to become (and who, by the
grace of our baptisms, already are) friends of God. We friends
of God do not begin this Gospel with a simple, bold, declarative

statement as in Mark's Gospel, or in the vastness of space and time as in John's Gospel, or within the rich history of Israel as in Matthew's Gospel. Although like Saint Matthew's Gospel, Saint Luke's begins with a genealogy, it is a genealogy that is much more inclusive. Matthew's genealogy begins with Abraham, whereas Luke's version traces back to Adam, the father of all mankind, thus signifying that Christ was born not just for the Children of Israel but for all people. Luke's Gospel makes explicit what the infancy narratives of Matthew's Gospel imply with the presence of the Magi, those astrologers from far-off, Gentile lands — namely, that Jesus' birth is for everybody — the rich and the poor, the Jews and the non-Jews, even the Samaritans, a group considered by the Jewish people to be ritually impure. It is also called the "Gospel of the poor" because Luke (who is traditionally considered to have been a physician) depicts Jesus (who is the Divine Physician) as having a special love and devotion to the sick and the poor.

Saint Luke offers us rich parables that differ largely in style and content from those of Saint Matthew. In fact, no less an authority than the British novelist Charles Dickens described one of Saint Luke's parables, that of the prodigal son, as the greatest short story ever written.

This Gospel is considered to be the Gospel of Our Blessed Virgin Mother, Mary. It is thought that Our Lady was the one who told Luke details that only a mother could know, intimate details about the family history and background of her side of the family. Luke's Gospel includes the story of the Lord's infant cousin, John the Baptist (note that only this Gospel mentions the physical kinship between Jesus and Saint John the Baptist).

What might be most interesting in this Gospel is the role of women. In addition to the presence of Mary and her cousin, Saint Elizabeth, the Lord Jesus enjoys plenty of friendships — real, honest, good, happy, healthy, holy, relationships — with women. He loves, in the purest sense of that word, his dear friends Martha and Mary; he loves his friend Mary of Magdala, out of whom he cast seven demons; he loves the women who are his disciples and who support his mission. These women who follow Jesus are not apostles; that is very clear. They are not part of the apostolic band. And that's okay. They are disciples of the Lord and have a very special place in the Church.

There is so much more that I could write in appreciation of this Gospel. Here, I've intended only to introduce some themes, to draw attention to things we can listen for when we hear this Gospel proclaimed in Mass. What a gift we have in all the Gospels, but especially in Saint Luke's, the Gospel with the details that only a mother could know, the Gospel of mercy (look to Luke 15:11–32 — the parable of the prodigal son *and* of the merciful father), the Gospel of the poor, the Gospel of the women, the Gospel of the Gentiles — indeed, the Gospel of the Lord!

> Lord God, who chose Saint Luke to reveal by his preaching and writings the mystery of your love for the poor, grant that those who already glory in your name may persevere as one heart and one soul and that all nations may merit to see your salvation. Through our Lord Jesus Christ, your Son, who lives and reigns with you in the unity of the Holy Spirit, one God, for ever and ever.[1]

John's Gospel: An Appreciation

During each level of formation as a seminarian, I would pray with a particular Gospel, and at each level (high school, college, and major seminary), a different Gospel would become my favorite. Perhaps this is the result of being taught to pray with Scripture at an early age, but I found that each Gospel, with its individual portrayal of the Lord Jesus, attracted me at different points in my life. When I was in the high school seminary, I loved Luke, with all its stories and history. When I was in the college seminary, I adored Mark, with its blunt simplicity. When I was in the major seminary, I could not get enough of John's Gospel, to the point of writing my licentiate thesis on the story of the raising of Lazarus in John 11:1–44. When I was a younger priest, I prayed alongside the rich, rabbinical Jesus and the sense of connectedness to the past that Matthew's Gospel offered. These days, as I serve in Rome as a seminary formator and professor, all of the Gospels have increased in their appeal to me, although recently I have begun to pray most explicitly with John's Gospel again.

> **Saint John's is the most sophisticated of all the Gospels, linguistically, philosophically, and theologically.**

Let's go through this last of the Gospels to be written, shall we? Saint John's is the most sophisticated of all the Gospels, linguistically, philosophically, and theologically. Like Mark's Gospel, it has no infancy narrative; there is no story of the birth of Christ. Instead, it is set up completely differently from all of the other Gospels.

Matthew, Mark, and Luke are what we call the Synoptic Gospels. The word "synoptic" comes from the Greek, meaning "to look together," and indeed that is the case with these three Gospels. All three more or less follow a similar structure. John's Gospel is an entirely different creature. It starts not with a genealogy of Jesus' human ancestry, as Matthew and Luke do, but with a beautiful, poetic prologue set in the vastness of all eternity. It is very different from the beginning of Mark's Gospel, which is so blunt and direct.

Why is this Gospel so different from the others? Like each of the others, John's was written in a particular time period and for a particular audience; yet it is also different because it reflects one of the first times that the Church used not just the language, but also the style, of another culture. It is Hellenic, or Greek, in its style.

After we encounter, in the vastness of eternity, the mystery that is the Trinity, we turn to the figure of John the Baptist, the last and the greatest of the prophets. He is a model of humility who knows who he is and what he's intended to be and to do. John knows that, as great as he is, he is not the Messiah. His job is simply to point to the one who is coming after him.

The Gospel is traditionally broken into two parts — chapters 1–11 are called the Book of Signs, while chapters 12–21 are called the Book of Glory. I particularly love praying with the Book of Signs. In John's Gospel, the acts of Jesus that in the other Gospels are called miracles are called "signs." For the sake of simplicity, I'll suffice it to say that these signs that Jesus performs in this first part of John's Gospel get bigger and bigger, each one pointing to the reality that is right in front of the people of Jesus' day — namely, that this man is the Messiah. The signs grow from the wedding feast at Cana in chapter 2, to the various healings performed by the Lord, to the crucial moment in the Bread of Life Discourse where Jesus sets forth a radical truth and loses so many of his followers, to the culmination of all these signs — the raising of Lazarus in chapter 11. It is in this chapter that we see the Lord Jesus at his most human, in weeping deeply for his friend Lazarus, and at his most divine (until, of course, we read of his own resurrection), in raising Lazarus, who was four days dead, to life.

The chapters that constitute what is called the Book of Glory give us the story of the Lord's paschal mystery — his Passion, death, and resurrection — beginning with the Last Supper. In the Last Supper, John emphasizes the washing of the feet — though recall that he also includes the Bread of Life Discourse earlier in the Gospel, where he gives us a rich, beautiful theology of the Eucharist. John 20:30 gives us the simple, clear reason why this Gospel was written: "Now Jesus did many other signs in the presence of the disciples, which are not written in this book; but these are written that you may believe that Jesus is the Christ, the Son of God, and that believing you may have life in his name." This is what this beautiful Gospel is all about!

The Gospel's last chapter serves as its epilogue, and in a simple closing sentence, Saint John describes how deep this Gospel really is: "There are also many other things that Jesus did, but if these were to be described individually, I do not think the whole world would contain the books that would be written" (Jn 21:25, NABRE).

A Reflection on the "Last Gospel"

One of the joys I have in my life as a priest who is assigned as a formator and as a theology professor is learning from my students. While I was writing this book, I was blessed to offer two theological seminars in the field of dogmatic theology for Rome's Pontifical Gregorian University. The Gregorian allows the seminar professor a tremendous amount of flexibility in what he or she will offer for his or her students' reading and reflection. And I must admit that a great benefit for both professor and student is that the language of instruction is English, not Italian! In one of those two classes, I taught nine students from around the world, from countries such as Tanzania, Scotland, England, and Croatia. All were seminarians, some religious, others diocesan, and each of them came from radically different experiences of the Church and the world. It was a delight to be their professor and, as we read Joseph Ratzinger's *Introduction to Christianity*, I learned what theology is like through an international, and very Catholic, perspective. Remember, the word "catholic" itself means "universal"!

In the other seminar for the Gregorian, I taught twelve students, all seminarians for dioceses throughout the United States and Australia. These men are very intelligent and extremely insightful in their knowledge of philosophy. It is one of my goals to assist these young seminarians, who are just beginning their study of theology, to make the subtle transition from philosophy, the indispensable handmaiden of theology, to theology itself. It is fascinating to see the gradual appreciation that comes about in their intellectual formation when they pass from a fideism (an error that elevates faith in importance against reason) or a rationalism (a similar error that stresses reason to the detriment of faith) to the balanced understanding of theology and philosophy such as is found in Pope Saint John Paul II's magnificent encyclical *Fides et Ratio* (1998). One of the readings we studied together as a point of synthesis was Pope Saint John Paul II's masterpiece *Veritatis Splendor* (1993). This encyclical uses the fonts of Divine Revelation — Sacred Scripture and Sacred Tradition — wisely and properly, and navigates well among the different theological disciplines of morals, dogmatics, fundamentals, biblical studies, and patristics.

Some of my students, during their philosophy training at the Catholic University of America, were blessed to have a professor whom I never learned from or met — Monsignor Robert Sokolowski. I avidly read Monsignor Sokolowski's book *The God of Faith and Reason* (1982) as a seminarian many years ago, as well as his text on *Eucharistic Presence* (1994), and I found them to be seminal in the formation of my own theological method.

Sokolowski also has a book titled *Christian Faith & Human Understanding: Studies on the Eucharist, Trinity, and the Human Person.* I am very grateful to a former student of mine who introduced me to a chapter in this wonderful text, "Praying the Canon of the Mass." At the end of the chapter, Monsignor Sokolowski writes:

> I would like to close these reflections on the prayers of
> the priest by making a suggestion for thanksgiving after

Mass. In the old rite, the prayer called the *Placeat* and
the Prologue to Saint John's Gospel were said toward the
end of the Mass, before and after the final blessing and
dismissal. This prayer and Gospel are not used in the
new rite, but they can well be recommended as private
prayers of the priest after the Mass is over. In the *Placeat*
the priest prays that the sacrifice he has just offered be
pleasing to the Holy Trinity and that it be beneficial for
himself and those for whom it was offered. In the Prologue to Saint John's Gospel we recall the preexistence
of the Word as God with God, the coming of the Word
as life and light for men, the acceptance and rejection of
the Word, the contrast between John the Baptist and Jesus, and the Incarnation among us. These prayerful and
biblical thoughts are appropriate as part of the priest's
thanksgiving after the sacrifice of the Mass and the reception of communion. The fact that they were included
in the Mass in the old rite shows that their suitability for
the Eucharist was recognized in earlier ages. Using them
as prayers of thanksgiving will remind us of the continuity between the old rite of the Mass and the new.[2]

I would like to add to Monsignor Sokolowski's thoughts and suggest that praying the Prologue to the Gospel of Saint John as a
private prayer of thanksgiving after Mass is appropriate not only
for priests but for all Catholics.

Why was this portion of the Gospel read not just at Christ-
mas Mass, as is the case in the current rite, but at the conclusion
of every Mass? I believe it was for one reason: to remind us —
who have just received the Body of Christ — to become, in our
words and in our deeds, him whom we have just received. We are
called to make incarnate, to make flesh, the Eternal Word who
was from the beginning, allowing him to live in us, just as he did

in the spotless, immaculate womb of the Blessed Virgin Mary.

> *We are called to make incarnate, to make flesh, the*
> *Eternal Word who was from the beginning, allowing*
> *him to live in us, just as he did in the spotless,*
> *immaculate womb of the Blessed Virgin Mary.*

Making a private thanksgiving prayer reflecting deeply on the mystery of Christ, who is living inside each of us after the reception of holy Communion, is an essential aspect of the Mass. Sadly, it is often neglected in our parishes today. How quickly some parishioners run out of Mass after they have received holy Communion! How odd it appears in some parishes when some parishioners actually stay in the church after Mass to make a prayer of thanksgiving! We have become, in some churches, all too used to the church being a place of conversation after the conclusion of a Sunday Mass.

A good spiritual practice to encourage in our parishes is to make an act of thanksgiving to the Lord after Mass. Of course, one can also use the time of silence after Communion (the time between the ending of the Communion antiphon or Communion hymn and the praying of the collect after Communion by the priest), which is an essential part of the Mass, to kneel or sit quietly, reflecting on what has just occurred to us at that moment of the Mass.

At that moment, with the Lord living in us, we are as close to heaven as we are ever going to be on this earthly plane of existence. The ultimate gift has been given to us. The Word, who was from the beginning, the One through whom all things were made, the One who is Life, Jesus, is living inside of us.

Jean-Jacques Olier, SS (1608–1657), the founder of the Sulpicians, expressed this sentiment beautifully. He writes: "O Jesus, living in Mary, come and live in your servants, in the spirit of holiness, in the fullness of your power, in the perfection of your ways, in the truth of your virtues, in the communion of your mysteries. Rule over every adverse power, in your Spirit, for the glory of the Father. Amen."[3]

When we pray the words of John's Prologue, they powerfully remind us of the reality of what is occurring spiritually (and, indeed, even physically) to us. We are given hope when we pray these words of the Prologue: "And this life was the light of the human race; / the light shines in the darkness, / and the darkness has not overcome it" (Jn 1:4–5, NABRE). The world can be a dark place. There are problems, there are difficulties, there are fears and anxieties, but the Lord is right there with us, our food for the journey. That light has conquered the darkness of our world.

When we pray the words of the Prologue, they remind us that, just as the Eternal, Incarnate Word came to his own and was rejected, so, too, can we be rejected, even by our own families and friends, when we try to become him whom we receive. This is a painful reality for all too many people today. However, we have confident assurance that the Lord is right there with us, in our midst: "But to those who did accept him he gave power to become children of God, to those who believe in his name, who were born not by natural generation nor by human choice nor by a man's decision but of God" (Jn 1:12–13, NABRE). In the Eucharist, we are made one Body in Christ.

Consider using the Prologue of John's Gospel as part of your private meditation after Mass. I am very grateful to my student who introduced me to Monsignor Sokolowski's thoughts on it, and for his wisdom concerning many things, especially the Eucharist:

> In the beginning was the Word,
> and the Word was with God,
> and the Word was God.

He was in the beginning with God.
All things came to be through him,
    and without him nothing came to be.
What came to be through him was life,
    and this life was the light of the human race;
    the light shines in the darkness,
    and the darkness has not overcome it.

A man named John was sent from God. He came for testimony, to testify to the light, so that all might believe through him. He was not the light, but came to testify to the light. The true light, which enlightens everyone, was coming into the world.

He was in the world,
    and the world came to be through him,
    but the world did not know him.
He came to what was his own,
    but his own people did not accept him.

But to those who did accept him he gave power to become children of God, to those who believe in his name, who were born not by natural generation nor by human choice nor by a man's decision but of God.

And the Word became flesh
    and made his dwelling among us,
    and we saw his glory,
    the glory as of the Father's only Son,
    full of grace and truth. (John 1:1–14, NABRE)

Learning to Appreciate the Fathers of the Church

Many years ago, when I entered the college level seminary in

Douglaston, New York, I was handed a copy of *Christian Prayer*, the one-volume version of the Liturgy of the Hours.[4] As a freshman in college, I found this little book to be a mystery. For starters, it had too many ribbons. (I think that people who are first exposed to the Divine Office on an app are so spoiled, yet I do really appreciate the iBreviary!) And at the end of my freshman year of college, what a day it was when I bought my copy of the four-volume Liturgy of the Hours. For me, as a nineteen-year-old, it was a real sign of commitment to my vocation. I felt like I was entering the big leagues!

Together, our small community living in the College House of Formation learned to pray Lauds, Vespers, and what quickly became my favorite, Compline. At this early stage in formation, Midday Prayer was not yet prayed in common, nor was the Office of Readings. However, in an adaptation to the rubrics of the Liturgy of the Hours, we would, when we prayed Lauds together, also read as a community the second reading from the Office of Readings. I immediately fell in love with the Office of Readings. It introduced me to a whole new world — a world populated by the heroes of the great Sacred Tradition of the Church, the Fathers of the Church.

Falling in Love with the Fathers

Over that summer between my freshman and sophomore years of college, I found in a used book store a copy of a really great old book, published in 1958, that helped me to grow to know the Fathers of the Church even more: *The Fathers without Theology: The Lives and Legends of the Early Church Fathers* by Marjorie Strachey. The Fathers of the Church quickly became trusted guides. I urge you to get to know saints, pastors, and teachers such as Justin, Clement, Jerome, Ambrose, Augustine, John Chrysostom, Athanasius (the "Hammer of the Heretics"), Maximus, Basil, Gregory of Nyssa, Gregory Nazianzen, Hilary, Cyril of Alexan-

dria (on whose feast day I was ordained a priest), the great popes
Leo and Gregory, Bede the Venerable, Cyprian of Carthage, and
Origen.[5]

All of Theology Is Kept in the Fathers

Another priest whom I really respect and who serves as a professor in a seminary told me many years ago: "All of the answers
to the problems of theology today can be found in the first seven
ecumenical councils. That's where theology ends!" I don't entirely
agree with his statement, but he's not completely wrong. My own
specialty is in contemporary theology. I wrote my doctorate on
the twentieth-century theologians John Courtney Murray and
Bernard Lonergan. They are, to me, fascinating thinkers and I
am very glad that I studied them. However, the older I get and the
more I read and study, the more I realize that all theology is built
on the firm foundation that is Divine Revelation's fonts, Sacred
Scripture and Sacred Tradition. Even the thinkers that I ask my
students to read in their introductory theology class are mostly
from the *ressourcement*[6] period, men such as de Lubac, Congar,
Balthasar, Daniélou, and Ratzinger, all of whom ask their readers
to go back to the Fathers.

> *Getting to know the great patristic era can help us
> understand the present age.*

Getting to know the great patristic era can help us understand the
present age. In his introduction to Athanasius's *The Incarnation*,
C. S. Lewis writes:

> This mistaken preference for the modern books and this
> shyness of the old ones is nowhere more rampant than
> in theology. Wherever you find a little study circle of
> Christian laity you can be almost certain that they are

studying not Saint Luke or Saint Paul or Saint Augustine or Thomas Aquinas or Hooker or Butler, but M. Berdyaev or M. Maritain or M. Niebuhr or Miss Sayers or even myself.

Now this seems to me topsy-turvy. Naturally, since I myself am a writer, I do not wish the ordinary reader to read no modern books. But if he must read only the new or only the old, I would advise him to read the old. And I would give him this advice precisely because he is an amateur and therefore much less protected than the expert against the dangers of an exclusive contemporary diet. [Emphasis added.]

A new book is still on its trial and the amateur is not in a position to judge it. It has to be tested against the great body of Christian thought down the ages, and all its hidden implications (often unsuspected by the author himself) have to be brought to light.

Often it cannot be fully understood without the knowledge of a good many other modern books. *If you join at eleven o'clock a conversation which began at eight you will often not see the real bearing of what is said. Remarks which seem to you very ordinary will produce laughter or irritation and you will not see why — the reason, of course, being that the earlier stages of the conversation have given them a special point.* [Emphasis added.][7]

Yes, if we rely solely on theology written in the past few years, as good as some of it is, we will be no different than Lewis's conversationalist chiming in late in the conversation. We risk building our houses on sand, surely doomed to fail. I was a college seminarian when that true gift of Saint John Paul II that is the *Catechism of the Catholic Church* was released in 1992. I explicitly recall a theology professor bemoaning the fact that the new *Cat-*

echism had no quotes from any twentieth-century theologians. I remember thinking, even as a young student, that these theologians had not yet stood the test of time. And all of the truly great Catholic theologians of the twentieth and twenty-first centuries rely on the Fathers of the Church, along with Sacred Scripture, as the basis for their theology. You can't really do Catholic theology without them!

Learning from the Fathers

We need to go back to the Fathers to learn from them. Do we think we have troubles today between the Church and culture? Do we think we live in a world of confused theology and poor pastoral praxis? Go back and study the Fathers. They lived through difficult times, and they guided the Church as lights in an age of darkness. Read the Fathers, not just about them![8]

So with no further ado and in no particular order, I would like to present ten reasons why I believe that all of us should read the Fathers of the Church:

1. *The Fathers were mostly pastors, not academics.* There is an old definition of religion as "man's response to God as God reveals himself to man." The Fathers were living their Christian lives in response to what they were experiencing in the Church and in the culture of their day. Their writings were not coming from a tenured professorship — they were trying to serve the flock with whom God had blessed them.

2. *The Fathers teach us to love the Church.* The Second Vatican Council's *Lumen Gentium* offered — as its primary image for the Church — the Church as the People of God. Pope Pius XII, in his encyclical *Mys-*

tici Corporis, offers us the image of the Church as
the Body of Christ. The pope and the Fathers of the
Second Vatican Council did not invent these images.
They come not only from Sacred Scripture but also
from the early Fathers. In one of the passages that I
consider to be among the most beautiful in the patristic corpus, "On the Unity of the Church," Saint
Cyprian of Carthage (c. 200–258) writes: "He can
no longer have God for his Father who has not the
Church for his mother." The Church is our mother
— and we should exhibit the same devotion toward
the Church that we do toward Mother Mary.

3.   *The Fathers teach us what it means to be human, truly human.* I offer again the beautiful words of Saint
Cyprian describing the sinful culture of his day, of
which he was part before his conversion and his
baptism: "I was still lying in darkness and gloomy
night, wavering hither and thither, tossed about on
the foam of this boastful age, and uncertain of my
wandering steps, knowing nothing of my real life,
and remote from truth and light … but after that, by
the help of the water of new birth, the stain of former
years had been washed away, and a light from above,
serene and pure, had been infused into my reconciled heart."[9]

Many of us know about the great conversion
of Saint Augustine of Hippo (354–430), which he
gloriously presents in his *Confessions*.[10] But all of
the Fathers lived in the world, the fallen world, and
they each came to the conclusion — because they
fell in love with Christ in his Church — that they
had to convert to the truth, goodness, beauty, love,

and knowledge that is Christ. They teach us to put to death the old man of sin and to embrace the new man in Christ. Consider the words of Saint Irenaeus (c. 130–c. 202): *"Gloria Dei est vivens homo"* ("The glory of God is man fully alive").[11]

4.   *The Fathers teach us to be friends with God (and with each other).* The Fathers of the Church were truly men striving for holiness. Being fully alive as Saint Irenaeus means it, means more than just "living life to the full." It's not about self-fulfillment. It's about living the life of Christ. As Christ, fully man, fully God, was capable of beautiful friendships, so too were the Fathers. Read the words of Saint Gregory Nazianzen (329–390) about his dear friend Saint Basil: "Such was the prelude to our friendship, the kindling of that flame that was to bind us together. In this way we began to feel affection for each other. When, in the course of time, we acknowledged our friendship and recognized that our ambition was a life of true wisdom, we became everything to each other: we shared the same lodging, the same table, the same desires, the same goal. Our love for each other grew daily warmer and deeper."

Being fully alive, as Saint Irenaeus means it, means more than just "living life to the full." It's not about self-fulfillment. It's about living the life of Christ.

He continues:

We seemed to be two bodies with a single spirit. Though we cannot believe those who claim that everything is contained in everything, yet you must believe that in our case each of us was in the other and with the other.

Our single object and ambition was virtue, and a life of hope in the blessings that are to come; we wanted to withdraw from this world before we departed from it. With this end in view we ordered our lives and all our actions. We followed the guidance of God's law and spurred each other on to virtue. If it is not too boastful to say, we found in each other a standard and rule for discerning right from wrong.

Different men have different names, which they owe to their parents or to themselves, that is, to their own pursuits and achievements. But our great pursuit, the great name we wanted, was to be Christians, to be called Christians.[12]

These two men had a friendship that was a gift from God, a gift that spurred them onward to be better: better men, better Christians. Some search their entire lives for such a friendship, one that makes the other a better person. Reading the Fathers can teach us to be better friends to God and to one another.

5.   *The Fathers teach us to be fearless.* These pastors, these shepherds of souls, were truly, utterly, entirely fearless. They feared God, not man, and suffered both physically and in their reputations for the true faith. For example, Saint Cyprian of Carthage was ordained a priest and bishop soon after his baptism, and he served as a bishop, caring pastorally for his flock, until he was martyred in A.D. 258. During the great persecutions of Christians under Emperor Decius, Cyprian, in exile, wrote pastoral letters instructing the people of God in Carthage. Under Em-

peror Valerian, Cyprian was condemned to death. Upon receiving his death sentence, he responded, *"Deo gratias!"* ("Thank God!"). Or let's examine the heroic life of Saint Maximus the Confessor (c. 580– 662). This great saint, in his battle against Monothelitism (a heresy that taught that Our Lord had two natures but only one [divine] will) had his tongue cut out and his right hand severed. It was done by the order of Emperor Constans II, and the goal was to deter Saint Maximus from defending orthodox truths of the Faith. These preachers were truly brave in their actions and in their faith — and they taught the truth no matter what opposition they faced. Would that my brother clerics and I all have that courage!

6.   *The Fathers teach us to love clear doctrine.* Saint Athanasius (296/8–373) faced what seemed to be an impossible situation. There was a priest from Alexandria in Egypt named Arius who really misinterpreted the Prologue of the Gospel of John. Arius taught that there was a God, and this uncreated God, who existed from all eternity, created only one thing — the Logos (the Word). This Logos (who could, according to Arius, also be called a God, or even the Son of God) then created all things. In Arius's teachings, there was no concept of the Most Blessed Trinity. And Jesus, according to Arius, was an intermediary figure, neither fish nor fowl, neither divine nor human. The sad thing was that many Christians believed Arius and were led away from the Catholic faith. Athanasius strove to teach the truths about Jesus Christ and the Trinity, and to keep the flock of Christ together, but unfortunately the large num-

ber of misled Christians included many bishops. It was truly *"Athanasius contra mundum"* ("Athanasius against the world"), but his ceaseless desire for clear doctrine led to the Council of Nicaea's Creed — which to this day is used by Christians throughout the world to profess the faith of the one, holy, catholic, and apostolic Church.

7. *The Fathers teach us to love the Blessed Virgin Mary.* The Fathers love the Mother of God. There was a heretic by the name of Nestorius who taught that Mary was only the *Christotokos* (Christ-bearer), not the *Theotokos* (God-bearer). In other words, he taught that Our Lady was not the Mother of God, as she only gave birth to the human nature of Jesus. Saint Cyril of Alexandria (c. 376–444) fought tirelessly against this tremendous theological error. In a letter correcting Nestorius, Cyril writes: "For our sake and for our salvation, he assumed his human nature into the unity of his Person and was born of a woman; this is why it is said that he was born according to the flesh."[13] (Cyril was able to preserve a proper understanding not only of Mary but also of Christ. Mary could not give birth to a nature — she gave birth to a Person, a Divine Person who has two natures, human and divine. There is no division in Our Lord between his humanity and divinity but perfect unity. This understanding is essential — salvation depends on the union of Jesus' two natures, human and divine, in his one Person.) Our Blessed Lady is an essential figure in salvation history and is worthy of the title of the Mother of God. We have the great Father of the Church, Cyril of Jerusalem (c.

313–386), to thank for clarifying this teaching.

8. *The Fathers teach us how to interpret Sacred Scripture.* Most of the literature we have from the Apostolic and post-Apostolic Fathers is their homilies, which offer some of the best biblical exegesis imaginable. Examine Saint Augustine's *Tractates on the Gospel of John*; the sections on the man born blind and the woman at the well are among his finest writings. A twentieth-century theologian, Cardinal Henri de Lubac, basing his thinking on the Fathers of the Church, taught in his work *Medieval Exegesis* that, in order to understand Sacred Scripture, we need to know that it has four senses. These are the literal, the allegorical, the moral, and the anagogical senses. The *Catechism of the Catholic Church* cites a medieval couplet attributed to Augustine of Dacia (d. 1282) that summarizes these four senses: "*Lettera gesta docet, quid credas allegoria, / moralis quid agas, quo tendas anagogia*" ("The Letter speaks of deeds; Allegory to faith; / The Moral how to act; Anagogy our destiny.") (CCC 118). Here is de Lubac's translation: "The letter teaches events; allegory what you should believe; morality teaches what you should do, anagogy what mark you should be aiming for."[14] The Fathers of the Church are among the best scriptural exegetes in history.

9. *The Fathers teach us how to be saints.* They were all about holiness of life and, as true pastors of the Faith, are all about getting their flocks to heaven along with them. In his classic text *Jesus of Nazareth*, Pope Benedict XVI states: "The saints are the true interpreters

of Holy Scripture. The meaning of a given passage of the Bible becomes most intelligible in those human beings who have been totally transfixed by it and lived it out."[15] Each of the Fathers, in his own way, taught about Christians partaking of, and participating in, the divinity of Christ. Saint Ignatius of Antioch writes:

> I do also love the prophets as those who announced Christ, and as being partakers of the same Spirit with the apostles. For as the false prophets and the false apostles drew [to themselves] one and the same wicked, deceitful, and seducing spirit; so also did the prophets and the apostles receive from God, through Jesus Christ, one and the same Holy Spirit, who is good, and sovereign, and true, and the Author of [saving] knowledge. For there is one God of the Old and New Testament, "one Mediator between God and men," for the creation of both intelligent and sensitive beings, and in order to exercise a beneficial and suitable providence [over them]. There is also one Comforter, who displayed His power in Moses, and the prophets, and apostles.[16]

10. *The Fathers were treasured by one of the greatest saints and teachers.* At his essence, Saint Thomas Aquinas is, even more than a gifted philosopher, a brilliant commentator not only on Sacred Scripture but also

on Sacred Tradition. Stephen Beale, in his incredible article in the *National Catholic Register* "Which Church Fathers Most Influenced Saint Thomas Aquinas?"[17] breaks it all down for us clearly: Saint Augustine of Hippo is quoted by Saint Thomas in the *Summa Theologiae* 3,156 times! Here's the rest of Mr. Beale's analysis regarding how often Saint Thomas quotes various Church Fathers:

1. Gregory the Great — 761 times
2. Dionysius — 607
3. Jerome — 377
4. John Damascene — 367
5. John Chrysostom — 309
6. Ambrose — 284
7. Isidore — 162
8. Origen — 84
9. Basil — 56
10. Gregory of Nyssa — 53
11. Athanasius — 45
12. Cyril — 28

Wow! If the greatest mind that the Catholic Church and the Western world has ever produced is so devoted to the Fathers, why aren't we when we do theology?

The ten reasons offered above are merely a quick overview of these true theologians. What more can I say? I love the great Fathers of the Church, and you should, too. Please get to know and to love them. They inspired Thomas Aquinas, they inspired Pope Benedict XVI, and they surely will continue to inspire you and me.

Points to Remember

- Divine Revelation consists of Sacred Scripture and Sacred Tradition. Both are vital for an understanding of our faith in its fullness.
- Our study of the sources, both Sacred Scripture and Sacred Tradition, must inform our spiritual lives and our pastoral lives.
- Knowledge and love of the Fathers of the Church are essential for any serious study of theology.

Suggestions for Further Reading

For further reading concerning topics in this chapter, you might want to consult the following:

- Raymond E. Brown, *An Introduction to the New Testament* (New York/London/Toronto/Sydney/Auckland: Doubleday, 1997).
- Paul Haffner, *New Testament Theology: An Introduction* (Rome: Millstream Productions, 2006).
- Boniface Ramsey, *Beginning to Read the Fathers*, rev. ed. (Mahwah, NJ: Paulist Press, 2012).
- Christopher A. Hall, *Reading Scripture with the Church Fathers* (Westmont, IL: InterVarsity Press, 1998).

6

A Brief History of Theology

B efore we look at a brief history of theology, I'll take you along
on a personal excursion. One of the most unpleasant tasks of
my life was writing my doctoral thesis in theology. This had not
so much to do with my doctoral director, nor with the university,
nor even with my topic per se. Nor did it have to do with a lack of
love for academic work. In fact, I see my academic life as essential
to my own priestly ministry and as one of the greatest aids to my
spiritual life. No, the unpleasantness of my doctoral writing had
entirely to do with me wanting to write what I wanted to write,
with no desire to change the ideas that I had.

When I started my doctoral studies, the topic on which I
wanted to write was an obscure one, to say the least — namely,
the function of philosophy in the Eucharistic theology of a female
Anglican theologian writing about the Real Presence of Christ. In
the university in which I was enrolled, I was working with a brilliant theologian who seemed to be speaking an entirely different
language than I was. My ideas were going in one direction, while
his advice to me was to go in a completely opposite direction. My
original topic was doomed, lost in a maze of my enthusiasm for a

topic that perhaps I did not fully understand the implications of in my own proposal.

Eventually, I switched universities, switched topics, and worked with a director who was a very "directive" thesis moderator — one who certainly had different ideas than I did and who challenged me again and again to see the bigger picture. It wasn't easy, this process of writing a thesis; at one point, I had a dissertation that was well over 800 pages. And in my enthusiasm and my own intellectual pride, I loved every single page of that version. Editing the work was like saying goodbye to dear friends — I could tell you where I was when I wrote each section of that thesis. However, at that length, my dissertation read like the phone book. It was filled with obscurities that fascinated me but, to be blunt, hindered the reader's comprehension of the topic itself — namely, the development of the theology of the twentieth-century theologian John Courtney Murray.[1]

The best advice I was ever given concerning the academic life came from a very well respected US Catholic Church historian. We were sitting in a café directly outside of the Pantheon in Rome where I was studying, and I was moaning about various picayune details that I felt were unfair in the process of writing my thesis. This historian looked at me and, with the great seriousness that can only come from one who has gone through a similar process of being a doctoral student, said: "Just get it done. Sit in the chair in front of the computer and write."

I was taken aback. I had expected some sage wisdom from a master, and all I received was "git 'er done." Then, having said that, this priest-professor gave me a comforting look and some more wise advice, quoting John's Gospel: "Do whatever he tells you" (Jn 2:5). The "he" in the sentence referred not only to the Lord but also to my dissertation director.

For too long in the process of writing, I had been "kicking against the goads" (Acts 26:14), wanting to do my own thing and not wanting to do what my director thought would be best for me. After speaking to the historian that night, I began to listen more carefully to my director.

After the doctoral defense, which was described by a priest friend of mine as "academic hazing" (and which was, to be very honest, the quickest ninety minutes of my life), my director met with me and offered me an observation. He stated that my interest was not so much in fundamental or dogmatic theology (which was what my newly granted degree was in) as much as it was in the history of theology. By that, he didn't mean Church history, but the history *of theology* — namely, the way that Catholic theology as a field has developed over the years. The more I study, the more I teach, the more I write, the more I realize that my doctoral director was absolutely correct.

Why the History of Theology?

As we have seen in previous chapters, theology is not philosophy — although philosophy is necessary in order to have the framework to "do theology." We have seen that reason is essential to the intellectual endeavor of theology, and that faith is key if it is to be *theology* and not simply an academic discipline like any other.

The history of theology is the history of how human beings in the Catholic Church have thought, and continue to think, about God and the things of God.

Despite the close relationship between philosophy and theology, it is crucial that we do not view the history of theology the way we view the history of philosophy. The history of theology is not just the history of ideas about God. It's so much more than that! It is the history of how human beings in the Catholic Church, a divinely inspired human institution, have thought, and continue to think, about God and the things of God.

In previous chapters, we have seen the vital role the Fathers of the Church (especially Saint Augustine of Hippo) and the Scholastics (particularly Saint Thomas Aquinas) have played in the history of theology. Now, we need to examine the history of Catholic theology in the modern and contemporary periods.

How should we begin this study of the history of theology? Now that the groundwork has been laid, let's examine a series of time periods in terms of theology, and how that theology was developed and perceived. As mentioned before, we'll want to keep in mind the significant roles that philosophy, politics, and culture play in our understanding of things. By this, I do not mean that the truths of the Faith fluctuate (on the contrary, they are unchanging); yet within the act of understanding (even within the act of understanding the loftiest theological teachings), our view occurs from within our own particular culture and historical vantage point.

Now, a word on how I have divided up the history of theology for this chapter. There are so many ways in which this could have been done, whether by schools of thought, dominant theological ideas, certain thinkers, or the papacy. I decided to let the Chair of Peter be the guide. My intention is to demonstrate how theology has grown and changed during the periods in which some of the popes served in the papacy. In order that this doesn't become a tome stretching from Saint Peter to Pope Francis, I have decided to focus on a few popes from the nineteenth and twentieth centuries.

Blessed Pope Pius IX — The First Modern Pope?

We'll begin with Pope Pius IX (reigned 1846–1878). He is on the path to sainthood and was beatified by Pope John Paul II in 2000. Some Church historians describe Pope Paul VI (1963–1978) as the "first modern pope," but I disagree. I give that title to Blessed Pope Pius IX. He is the first pope who had to deal with things not even Leo the Great faced in the fifth century when he had to deal with the invasions of Attila the Hun. The Huns at least shared with Leo a belief in the supernatural, whereas Pope Pius IX had to defend his flock and the Faith in an age that mocked the supernatural. In his writings, he addresses the unhealthy "isms" in the culture of the time: materialism, relativism, secularism, and modernism — each of which places the passing things of this earth above the things of God and the eternal. We Catholics are still facing this problem today. In this age of digital media and political correctness — an age that, as the late Cardinal Francis George put it, "permits everything and forgives nothing" — we can turn to two things that Pius IX himself relied upon: first, wisdom to read the signs of the times; and second, the quality of mercy.

In this age of digital media and political correctness, we can turn to two things that Pius IX himself relied upon: first, wisdom to read the signs of the times, and second, the quality of mercy.

What Can We Learn from Pius IX?

First, wisdom. His heroic sanctity and true wisdom are apparent when we look at the defining moments of his papacy. These include his foresight in declaring the dogma of the Immaculate Conception and in convening the First Vatican Council, which in 1870 defined papal infallibility in *Pastor Aeternus* (First Dogmatic Constitution on the Church of Christ) and examined the roots of Divine Revelation in *Dei Filius* (Dogmatic Constitution on the Catholic Faith). (It is of special note to those of us who are Americans that Piux IX also founded the North American College in Rome in 1859 and created the first American cardinal, Archbishop John McCloskey of New York.) He was a pope who was able to read the signs of the times for the sake of the truth, the Church, and the world.

As for his mercy, here's a small vignette about Pius IX. His longtime adversary was King Vittorio Emanuele II of Italy, against whom he issued edicts of interdict and excommunication. Upon learning of the king's illness and imminent death — and learning that the king wanted to "die a good Catholic" — the pope immediately rescinded the excommunication so that the king could receive the last rites. The king is buried in Santa Maria della Rotonda, better known as the Pantheon. The pope died one month after the king.

So What Does Pius IX Have to Do with Theology?

You may ask why I begin with Pius IX as the start of the modern/contemporary eras. This is a good question. I could have gone (and was tempted to go) back to the Reformation and the Counter-Reformation, or even to the Great Schism, but due to time constraints, I didn't. Instead, I have chosen to begin with Pius IX because he is a game changer, particularly with his *Syllabus of Errors* (1864). In my opinion, this work defines theology to this day. (In subsequent sections, you may wonder why I don't go too deeply into theology during the papacies of Benedict XV, Pius XI, John Paul I, and a few others. This is because theology during their reigns continued pretty much on the path it had been on with their predecessors.)

Pope Pius IX released an encyclical in 1864 titled *Quanta Cura* (Condemning Current Errors) with a famous appendix known as the *Syllabus of Errors*. At its essence, the *Syllabus* was a condemnation of eighty modern theses. The general American reaction to the *Syllabus of Errors* was not positive. Historian James Hennesey, SJ, describes the time period:

> The impact in the United States of Pius IX's 1864 *Syllabus of Errors*, in which Pius had left little doubt about his op-

position to most of the chief tenets of nineteenth-century liberalism, was muted since it appeared during the final winter of the Civil War. But, as [archbishop of Baltimore] Martin Spalding noted, "a howl of indignation" went up in the English and American press, which he attempted to calm with a pastoral letter explaining that Pius IX was concerned with "European radicals," and not with the American Constitution, separation of church and state as known in America, and liberty of conscience, worship, or the press as practiced in the United States.[2]

Archbishop John McCloskey of New York, one of the most prominent U.S. Catholic leaders at the time (and, as noted above, the first American cardinal), opined: "It is consoling to think and believe that our Holy Father has in all his official acts a light and guidance from on High — for according to all the rules of mere human prudence and wisdom the encyclical with its annex of condemned propositions would be considered ill-timed."[3]

And yet, despite the perception that the *Syllabus of Errors* was ill-timed at best and over-the-top at worst, there really was a problem in the Church. Modernism was a reality. Modernism attempted to modify the teachings of the Church to fit with modern ideas, and in Europe some Catholic theologians were modernists.[4] In the United States, there existed a more nuanced "Americanism,"[5] which Pope Leo XIII also addressed.

Pope Leo XIII — The Pope of Thomism

During the papacy of Leo XIII (1878–1903), many issues in theology had to be addressed. In 1879, he issued the encyclical *Aeterni Patris* (Of the Eternal Father), which was subtitled "On the Restoration of Christian Philosophy in Catholic Schools in the Spirit of the Angelic Doctor, Saint Thomas Aquinas." In the promulgation of this document, the pope wrote: "If anyone looks carefully at the bitterness of our times, and if, further, he considers earnestly the cause of those things that are done in public and private, he will discover with certainty the fruitful root of the evils which we greatly fear. The cause he will find to consist in this — evil teaching about things, human and divine, has come forth from the schools of the philosophers; it has crept into all orders of the State; and it has been received with the common applause of very many."[6]

It was Leo's wish, in the age of modernism, to reemphasize the thought of Saint Thomas Aquinas, which he felt was the most suitable philosophy and theology for the modern age. Jared Wicks highlights the importance of Saint Thomas, both overall and during the time of Pope Leo XIII, as he is a "model and norm of Catholic thought, for his works exemplify both the positive interrelation of reason and faith and the concern for an integrated study of doctrine that Vatican I had espoused."[7]

> *It was Leo's wish, in the age of modernism, to reemphasize the thought of Saint Thomas Aquinas, which he felt was the most suitable philosophy and theology for the modern age.*

The Creation of Manualism

There was, however, a major drawback to the universal application of the perennial wisdom of Saint Thomas. As Jared Wicks writes: "But every-day work in Catholic theology in the time between the two Vatican Councils was only rarely marked by the universal quest of wisdom characteristic of St. Thomas. The textbooks of theological instruction used in Catholic universities and seminaries were more influenced by the principles of [sixteenth-century neo-Scholastic theologian Melchior] Cano than by Aquinas."[8]

The encyclical ushered in the rise of a new form of Scholasticism, but it unfortunately also led to the rise of manualism. (It should be noted that Scholasticism is *not* the same as manualism. Too often, Scholasticism and manualism have been lumped together as a "big bad wolf" that held back the spirit of inquiry and theology during this period in history.) So what was manualism? It was a form of learning theology that, by and large, presented the truths of the Faith in a very digestible fashion.[9]

It's true that, unfortunately, the condemnation of modernism by the Vatican led to the codification of a manualistic theology and the predominance of a strict neo-Thomism that could be stifling.[10] And yet there really was no nefarious plot against the intellectual life. It is simply the fact that, when the Church acts, sometimes she overreacts. Many during this period relied heavily on sixteenth- and seventeenth-century commentaries on Aquinas.[11] Perhaps the most telling critiques of this thought came from Thomists themselves, such as Marie-Dominique Chenu (1895–1990), who adopted more modern methods of studying the thought of Saint Thomas and who considered some of the theology coming out of Rome at the time to be a miserable abuse of true Thomism.[12]

Other authors used pejorative terms such as "conclusion theology" to characterize the Roman theology of this time. It's a term that's meant to describe a theology so concerned with offering orthodox conclusions that it dispenses with providing arguments to support those conclusions. Such "conclusion theology" was described as reductionistic and self-referential.[13]

Did Theology Develop in the Time of Leo XIII?

There were some incredible moments of theology in this time. Pope Leo wrote an encyclical on social justice and economy that is completely applicable today: *Rerum Novarum* (On Capital and Labor), released in 1891. It addressed the working class and the relationship between workers and employees. He also released an incredible encyclical on the concept of divine inspiration in the Bible,

Providentissimus Deus (On the Study of Holy Scripture), in 1893. It described the methods for study of Scripture and the transmission and credibility of Divine Revelation in light of the present age.

Pope Saint Pius X — Continuing the Fight against Modernism

The saintly Pope Pius X (1903–1914) followed Leo XIII. He continued the reforms of his two immediate predecessors. In particular, he continued the battle against modernism, issuing an oath against modernism to be taken by pastors, theologians, and seminary professors. He also issued *Lamentabili Sane Exitu* (Syllabus Condemning the Errors of the Modernists) in 1907, which led to the encyclical *Pascendi Dominici Gregis* (Feeding the Lord's Flock), released in the same year.[14]

Venerable Pope Pius XII — Encouraging Theology *in* the Church

Following the pontificates of Pope Benedict XV (1914–1922) and Pope Pius XI (1922–1939), Pius XII became pope. This was a pope who supported theological studies, issuing such key encyclicals as *Mystici Corporis Christi* (On the Mystical Body of Christ), a groundbreaking document on ecclesiology, in 1943; *Mediator Dei* (Mediator of God), on the Sacred Liturgy, in 1947; and *Divino Afflante Spiritu* (Inspired by the Holy Spirit), described by some as the "Magna Carta of Scriptural studies," in 1943.[15] What all of these encyclicals had in common was a desire to return to the sources of Divine Revelation, namely Sacred Scripture and Sacred Tradition. In many ways, Pope Pius XII seemed in these encyclicals to be open to *ressourcement,* but he was also aware of how trends in theology can be misused. In 1950, he issued the encyclical *Humani Generis* (On Human Origin: Concerning Some False Opinions Threatening to Undermine the Foundations of Catholic Doctrine). He stated:

Everyone is aware that the terminology employed in the schools and even that used by the Teaching Authority of the Church itself is capable of being perfected and polished; and we know also that the Church itself has not always used the same terms in the same way. It is also manifest that the Church cannot be bound to every system of philosophy that has existed for a short space of time. Nevertheless, the things that have been composed through common effort by Catholic teachers over the course of the centuries to bring about some understanding of dogma are certainly not based on any such weak foundation. These things are based on principles and notions deduced from a true knowledge of created things. In the process of deducing, this knowledge, like a star, gave enlightenment to the human mind through the Church. Hence it is not astonishing that some of these notions have not only been used by the Ecumenical Councils, but even sanctioned by them, so that it is wrong to depart from them. (*Humani Generis* 16)

Humani Generis certainly affected the entire theological world — some argued that it stifled theological scholarship, and yet others argued that it did not come down hard enough on certain theologians. Describing the role of theology, Pius XII writes: "The most noble office of theology is to show how a doctrine defined by the Church is contained in the sources of revelation, ... in that sense in which it has been defined by the Church" (21).

> **The most noble office of theology is to show how a doctrine defined by the Church is contained in the sources of revelation, ... in that sense in which it has been defined by the Church.**
> (Pope Pius XII)

Pope Saint John XXIII — The Pope of the Council

Pope Saint John XXIII shocked the world at Saint Paul's Outside the Walls in 1959, with his call for a Second Vatican Council and a reformed Code of Canon Law. When he officially convoked the Second Vatican Council in the apostolic constitution *Humanae Salutis*, he spoke of how "the Church is witnessing a crisis underway in society" and suggested that such a crisis poses a challenge for theology: "It is a question in fact of bringing the modern world into contact with the vivifying and perennial energies of the gospel." He then spoke of how the Church needs to employ a method that is capable of relating the Gospel effectively to the times in which it finds itself. He stated: "We make ours the recommendation of Jesus that one should know how to distinguish the 'signs of the times' (Mt 16:4), and we seem to see now, in the midst of so much darkness, a few indications which auger well for the fate of the church and of humanity."[16]

The Signs of the Times

The pope reiterated this message in his opening address to the Council in 1962. Many of the subsequent decisions of the Council can be understood as a response to this request. The Council became devoted primarily to questions of ecclesiology and produced two of its four "constitutions" on this theme. *Lumen Gentium* (Light of Nations: Dogmatic Constitution on the Church) addressed the question of the mission of the Church *ad intra* (within the Church). *Gaudium et Spes* (Joy and Hope: Pastoral Constitution on the Church in the Modern World) addressed questions of the mission of the Church *ad extra* (outside the Church). This latter document opens with a reference to "the signs of the times": "The Church carries the responsibility of reading the signs of the times and of interpreting them in the light of the Gospel. ... In language intelligible to every generation, she should be able to answer the ever-recurring questions which people ask about the meaning of this present life and of the life to come."[17]

"Look, Judge, Act"

Pope John XXIII also introduced another set of terms to help explain the method he suggested was necessary for updating theology. In his social encyclical *Mater et Magistra* (Mother and Teacher), he spoke of the method "look, judge, act." He suggested that this method can help those promoting Catholic social teaching to relate it to the social contexts they wish to address: "There are three stages which should normally be followed in the reduction of social principles into practice. First, one reviews the concrete situation; secondly, one forms a judgment on it in the light of these same principles; thirdly, one decides what in the circumstances can and should be done to implement these principles. These are the three stages that are usually expressed in the three terms: look, judge, act."[18]

"Look, judge, act" proved to be a characteristic method of Vatican II as a whole. It was adopted, above all, in *Gaudium et Spes*. The document does not make explicit reference to the "look, judge, act" method, but is widely understood to have employed it.

Pope Saint Paul VI — Bringing the Council to Conclusion

John XXIII started the Council, but he did not finish it. With the exception of Pope John Paul I, no pope since the Second Vatican Council has been less known and less appreciated than Pope Saint Paul VI. Keep in mind that anyone born after 1978 has been alive only during the papacies of Pope Saint John Paul II, Pope Benedict XVI, and Pope Francis.

Pope Paul VI (1963–1978) is described by one biographer, Peter Hebblethwaite, as "the first modern pope."[19] In his own quiet way, Paul changed the way the world viewed the papacy. He was the first pope to travel to six continents and the first pope to visit the United States (Pius XII had extensively visited the United States in the 1930s when he was a cardinal). In 1965, Pope Paul became the first pontiff to address the United Nations, acting as an agent of peace. His words were: "No more war, never again war. Peace, it is peace that must guide the destinies of people and of all mankind." Paul survived an assassination attempt in the Philippines in 1970.

Pope Paul was not the Holy Father who initiated the Second Vatican Council, but it was he who saw it through to its conclusion — and it was he who had to shepherd the Church after the Council ended in the turbulent times of the 1960s and 1970s. Paul was seen by many as indecisive. He was viewed by some as a "liberal" who changed the Mass and downplayed papal attire and ceremonies. By others, he was considered someone who blocked the Church from going even further in its reforms. To think of him along these lines, however, is overly simplistic. Pope Paul VI wrote in a private note: "What is my state of mind? Am I Hamlet? Or Don Quixote? On the left? On the right? I do not think I have been properly understood. I am filled with 'great joy (*Superabundo gaudio*).' With all our affliction, I am overjoyed (2 Cor 2:4)."[20]

Pope Paul — The Steady Hand

Paul was the steady hand the Church needed at that time in her history. While he was open and attentive to the "signs of the times" (as his predecessor had urged), he also knew that not everything is negotiable and that there are some timeless truths that the Church must hold. He took a heroic stance in 1968 with the encyclical *Humanae Vitae* ("Of Human Life"), and his predictions regarding what a contraceptive mentality and practice would lead to have proven true. The contraceptive mentality has led to an abortive mentality, and respect for women and basic human civility have decreased tremendously over the past fifty years. Recall his words: "Love is total — that very special form of personal friendship in which husband and wife generously share everything, allowing no unreasonable exceptions and not thinking solely of their own convenience. Whoever really loves his partner loves not only for what he receives, but loves that partner for the partner's own sake, content to be able to enrich the other with the gift of himself."[21] Paul was also prescient in his 1967 encyclical *Populorum Progressio* (On the Development of Peoples), in which he emphasized that the world economy should attempt to benefit all mankind. His writings offer a rich, theological treasure for all Christians and for all the people of the world.

Theology after the Council

Here, it might behoove us to stop for a moment to examine some key terms and concepts in theology. Can we say that there has been one primary issue addressed in each decade following the Council? Perhaps. If so, we might say that in the 1960s it was the question of atheism and agnosticism; in the 1970s, ecclesiology; in the 1980s, Christology; in the 1990s, morals; and in the 2000s, dialogue with world religions. In the present decade, perhaps we could say we are focused on what it means to be the Church in an age where secularism has pounded the last nails in the coffin of Christendom — an age in which we need to restate our beliefs, and, perhaps in some instances, hit the restart button.

The key issue, as I see it, is whether we view Vatican II as being in continuity with tradition or as a rupture in tradition. The position that the Council was a rupture with tradition is actually two separate positions. On one side are those who think the Council was in error and separated the Church from her true self. On the other side are those who believe the Council cleared away obstacles from a stifling past so that the Catholic Church could begin "for real" in 1965.

Not Rupture, but Continuity in Tradition

I am strongly of the opinion that Vatican II is not a rupture, not a novelty. Rather, it builds on the foundation laid out by the Church since her inception. This is not to downplay the radicalness of Vatican II but instead to place the documents, which call for a return to the sources of Christianity, into proper context. As I tell my seminarians, "Know the documents. Do not permit anyone to interpret them for you." Know the importance of *Dei Verbum*, but see it as building on the foundation of Pius XII's *Divino Afflante Spiritu*. Recognize the importance of *Lumen Gentium*, but see it as arising from Pius XII's *Mystici Corporis*. Understand that *Sacrosanctum Concilium* is key, but notice that it flows from Pius XII's *Mediator Dei*. And all of these documents arise from ideas found within the Church's Tradition and Sacred Scripture.

> **Vatican II builds on the foundation laid out by the Church since her inception.**

Four Theological Camps

Before we go further and examine the three most recent popes, I would like to break contemporary Catholic theology into four camps. In doing so, I am limiting the thought of these theologians and, in a way, stereotyping them — but, for the sake of this section, I must attempt to categorize. I will use Dr. Tracey Rowland's divisions from her 2016 text *Catholic Theology*. There are, in her view, four camps: Concilium, Communio, Liberation Theology, and Thomism. Permit me to say something briefly about each of them.

1. *Concilium*

After the Second Vatican Council, some thinkers including Karl Rahner, Hans Kung, and Joseph Ratzinger came together to form a theological journal. They founded a journal titled *Concilium*, so named because they wished to live the spirit of the Second Vatican Council in their theology. To briefly describe their approach to theology, we could state that it has an anthropomorphic starting point, one that began from human experience; and a "Christology from below," one that began from an examination of Christ's human history.

2. *Communio*

Eventually, beginning around 1968, Joseph Ratzinger, after examining the situation of the world,[22] had a change of heart and began to see the limits of the Concilium approach. He, along with thinkers coming from the school of *ressourcement,* began a new journal, *Communio.* These *ressourcement* theologians included Henri de Lubac and Hans Urs von Balthasar. The overarching approach was more theocentric, beginning with God and the sources of Sacred Scripture and Sacred Tradition — and including (in some but not all cases) a "Christology from above" — that is, one that is developed from the concept of Christ as the preexistent Son of God who descended into the world to save it.[23]

3. Liberation Theology

Liberation theology operates from an approach that seeks to engage and enculturate the experiences of a people and shape theology around that. Theologians such as Gustavo Gutiérrez and Jon Sobrino are part of this "school." Its danger lies in the vision of the Kingdom of God as a political reality, one which can put the focus too much on the things of this world rather than on the things of the world to come. In short, where it can go wrong is in an overinvolvement in politics.

4. Thomism in the Contemporary Age

Finally, we have the perennial approach coming from Saint Thomas Aquinas. There are many different schools of thought regarding how to best interpret Saint Thomas — from a *ressourcement* approach (a return to examine Saint Thomas's original works in context) to a neo-Thomism flowing from the thought of, for example, Jacques Maritain, which seeks to address the dignity and nature of the human person and the rights and duties of citizens in society.[24]

Pope Saint John Paul II — A Master of Theology

In October 1978, the first non-Italian pope for many centuries was elected, and he brought a new and vibrant energy into the Church with him. Through sheer determination and the force of his personality and intellect, this Polish pope helped guide and direct the Church through world events.

One cannot help but recognize the masterful mind of Pope Saint John Paul II (1978–2005). His theology comes out of his philosophy. In his theology, he is a Thomist, but one needs to ask what type of Thomism he is engaging; it is a Thomism strongly allied with his philosophical personalism.[25]

In many ways, John Paul II was almost more of a philosopher than a theologian, although it is difficult to cast him in any one light. His thought was remarkably Christocentric and profoundly biblical. This is clear in the documents he released, such as *Redemptor Hominis* ("The Redeemer of Man") and *Salvifici Doloris* ("Redemptive Suffering").[26]

The State of Theology at the Beginning of John Paul II's Pontificate

In the early years of John Paul II's papacy, what was the state of theology? I see it as an age of clarifying Church teaching. To quote the late Monsignor George Kelly, it was a time of "keeping the Church Catholic with John Paul II."[27] The prior decades in the Church had been a time of asking many questions and reexamining theology in light of the modern world. Some theologians went so far in their thought that they ended up abandoning the core teachings of the Church (for example, some of the theologians who embraced the liberation theologians described above completely lost a sense of heaven as a supernatural reality and instead focused on earthy politics). John Paul II aided the Church in seeing the real issues at stake in her dialogues with the modern world. Note that this work of clarifying involved the writing of new editions of the *Catechism* and the Code of Canon Law.

> *John Paul II aided the Church in seeing the real issues at stake in her dialogues with the modern world.*

The Age of Certainty

One could break the pontificate of John Paul II up into two periods. As noted above, the earlier period in his papacy was one of clarification. I consider the second period (from 1992 to 2005) an age of further clarity that bore the fruit of security. The *Catechism of the Catholic Church* was first released in 1992. Some theologians considered it a threat and dismissed it as an attempt to stifle and manualize theology; yet nothing could be further from the truth. It was and is a clear guide to what we as Catholics believe and teach.

Let's consider some of the other works he released in this time period: for instance, 1992's *Pastores Dabo Vobis* ("I Will Give You Shepherds") gave the world a clear and precise way that the Church expected priests to be formed. Two documents (in addition to the *Catechism*) offered supreme examples of clarity in this time period. First, *Veritatis Splendor* ("The Splendor of Truth," 1993) gave a clear and beautiful articulation of the Church's moral norms in an age of moral relativism. Second, *Fides et Ratio* (1998) meditated upon and set guidelines for the proper use of philosophy and theology. For a young priest, these were days in which you had no doubt what it was that the Church taught!

The Age of Pope Benedict XVI

In the background of John Paul II's papacy was the brilliant figure of Cardinal Joseph Ratzinger. In 1981, Pope John Paul II, recognizing the academic brilliance and clarity of Cardinal Ratzinger, appointed him as the prefect of the Congregation for the Doctrine of the Faith, the office at the Vatican that seeks to clarify dogma and pastoral practices for the entire Catholic Church. Serving in this role for many years, the future pope became even more internationally known as a clear, concise, doctrinal theologian. The eight years of Benedict XVI's pontificate (2005–2013) can be broken into two periods.

The First Period of Pope Benedict: 2005–2008

Pope Benedict XVI chose the name "Benedict" because he wanted to save Europe,[28] much as earlier Church figures with the name "Benedict" had. Saint Benedict of Nursia (480–527), the founder of monasticism in the West, helped preserve Christianity and learning in the Dark Ages. Pope Benedict XV (1914–1922), the "pope of peace," reigned during the "war to end all wars," World War I.

It would be a mistake to label Pope Benedict XVI a mere "academic theologian"; he was passionate about the Faith and pastoral practice. Over time, many of those who initially dismissed him as merely a theological scholar came to see how his intellect (with his vast theological knowledge) combined with his deep life of prayer to inform his pastoral approach. This was truly Pope Benedict's gift to the Church in his years as pontiff.

First as Cardinal Ratzinger, and later as Pope Benedict XVI, he authored some of the most spiritual texts of the modern papacy, such as his contemporary classic series *Jesus of Nazareth* (2007–2012) and his text on prayer and the Sacred Liturgy, *The Spirit of the Liturgy* (2000). He also composed encyclicals that centered on one theme — friendship with the Lord Jesus Christ — as was demonstrated in his first encyclical, *Deus Caritas Est* ("God Is Love," 2005).

As we said at the very beginning of this book, theology is all about falling in love with Jesus, who is our friend. In friendships, the more we come to know others in time spent with them, the closer our friendships will be. Pope Benedict offers us the example of a man, a priest, a bishop, and a theologian who is a friend of Jesus and, in his writings, wants us to become friends with Jesus, too!

> **Pope Benedict offers us the example of a man, a priest, a bishop, and a theologian who is a friend of Jesus and, in his writings, wants us to become friends with Jesus, too!**

The Holy Father followed up *Deus Caritas Est* with *Spe Salvi* (On Christian Hope) in 2007. The third and final encyclical on the theological virtues, *Lumen Fidei* ("The Light of Faith"), was started by Pope Benedict and later completed by Pope Francis in 2013. Pope Benedict also published a social encyclical in 2009 titled *Caritas in Veritate*, in which he declares that love and truth must be intrinsically linked in the Christian life for the good of the world. He writes: "At the heart of the Church's social doctrine, it [love] must be linked to truth if it is to remain a force for good. Without truth, love can become an 'empty shell' to be filled with emotional influences which in the worst case can result in love turning into its opposite. Similarly, social action without truth can end up 'serving private interests and the logic of power'" (*CV* 3).

The Second Period of Pope Benedict: 2008–2013

In 2007, Benedict began to implement in the liturgy ideas he had first expressed in his book *The Spirit of the Liturgy* (2000).[29] In the life of the Church, her theology is always seen concretely in her liturgy. While Pope John Paul II had focused on clarifying the teachings of the Church by releasing a new and refined version of the catechism, Pope Benedict turned to the liturgy as a teaching tool. For example, he refined some parts of the English version of the Mass so that it would more clearly convey Church teaching. The Nicene Creed, for instance, underwent some revisions of terms, such as the Lord Jesus Christ being "consubstantial with the Father" (rather than "one in being with the Father" as the earlier English version stated) and "incarnate of the Virgin Mary" (rather than "born of the Virgin Mary"). These revisions assisted in clarifying theological uncertainties.

Pope Francis — A Complicated Theologian

On March 13, 2013, Cardinal Jorge Mario Bergoglio was elected the 265th Supreme Pontiff of the Roman Catholic Church. It is of note that this pope is not an academic "doctor of theology," and no one is asking him to be. Cardinal Bergoglio began a doctorate on the thought of Romano Guardini, but he never completed it. It is difficult to pinpoint any one theological school, or a particular theologian, as a main guide to his thought. While Thomism and personalism heavily influenced John Paul II, and Augustinianism and the Communio school did the same for Pope Benedict, the influences on Pope Francis are eclectic.

Pope Francis — A Theology of the People

Juan Carlos Scannone, a former professor of Pope Francis's, became an important interpreter of the pope. Scannone states that in order to understand Francis, one must come to an understanding of the "theology of the people" that was prevalent in Argentina after Vatican II.[30] Various commentators have noted that although the bishops of Argentina did not per se contribute a great deal to the proceedings of the Second Vatican Council, they quickly implemented the Council's pastoral and ecumenical teachings. In this matter, they were assisted by an interdisciplinary group of Catholic intellectuals who articulated a "theology of the people." The theology of the people derives its roots from *Lumen Genti-*

um's concept of the Church as the "People of God."[31] Scannone notes that what separated the Argentinian school from the rest of Latin American liberation theology was the fact that the Argentinians' focus was "socio-cultural" (that is, using the teachings of the Church as an impetus to improve societal conditions) rather than "socio-economic" (that is, looking to change structures of government and politics) as was the case elsewhere.[32]

The aim of the theology of the people is to create an alternate situation for people — one that, following the example of Christ, gives loving and careful consideration to the poor, keeping in mind that poverty is the life situation of many Argentinians. The focus is placed on culture and the values needed in evangelizing the culture. Popular piety, for example, plays an important role in creating the ecclesial and social identity of a people.

In living out his papacy, Francis has emphasized community as the primary image. The Church as community has concrete implications: "How important it is that the voice of every member of society be heard, and that a spirit of open communication, dialogue and cooperation be fostered. It is likewise important that special concern be shown for the poor, the vulnerable and those who have no voice, not only by meeting their immediate needs but also by assisting them in their human and cultural advancement."[33]

Various commentators note that prior to his becoming pope, Francis played an important role in persuading the bishops of Latin America to adopt the approach of a theology of the people. In 2007, as an archbishop, he led his fellow bishops during a portion of one of their general assemblies, held in Aparecida, Brazil. Regarding the work and publications that came out of this assembly, one author notes: "Commentators agree that Aparecida has a distinctively Argentinian theological tone, placing less emphasis on differences of economic class and employing a vocabulary of 'inculturation,' discussing the strengths and weaknesses of the popular piety of the poor, the experience of indigenous peoples, of women, and of urban dwellers. Also noteworthy is the fact that some non-Argentinian liberation theologians praised the Aparecida document and acknowledged that their own thinking had undergone a maturing process over the decades."[34]

The Practical Theologian

The Holy Father has said that the American Jesuit John Navone's (1930–2016) 1974 book *Triumph through Failure* (also published as *A Theology of Failure*) is one of the most influential books he has ever read. The pope states: "Patience is a theme that I have pondered over the years after my having read the book of John Navone, an Italian American author, with the striking title, *A Theology of Failure*, in which he explains how Jesus lived patiently."[35] In the experience of limits, Pope Francis adds: "Patience is forged in dialogue with human limitations. There are times when our lives do not call so much for our doing as for enduring, for bearing up with our own limitations and those of others. Patience accepts the fact that it takes time to develop and mature. Living with patience allows for time to integrate and shape our lives."[36]

> *Pope Francis is a pastor par excellence who uses an inductive method to approach each issue he encounters theologically.*

If we combine some of the insights outlined above with his experience of being a Jesuit from Argentina who served as provincial superior during a particularly difficult period, we might begin to understand Pope Francis. The Holy Father is a pastor par excellence who uses an inductive method to approach each issue he encounters theologically.

Two Periods of Pope Francis

As I did for his two immediate predecessors, I find it helpful to divide Pope Francis's reign (thus far) into two periods: the first, 2013–2015, and the second from 2015 to the present. I think we were getting used to Francis in those early days, and he was getting used to us. Also, he was wrapping up some of Benedict's work, especially *Lumen Fidei*, mentioned earlier. It is not unusual for a pope to complete an encyclical begun by his predecessor. What is unusual is for the pope to speak so freely and openly about it. Pope Benedict began this encyclical, and after his resignation on February 11, 2013, his successor, Pope Francis, took the document, amended it, and added his own thoughts.

It is amusing for those who have read Pope Benedict's works and listened to Pope Francis's talks and homilies to try to discern what parts were written by Benedict and what parts were written by Francis. My own opinion is that the document as it appears is mostly the work of Benedict, up until section 50. However, it ultimately does not matter in the least. Its consistency, and the unity of the two minds and hearts of our pope and pope emeritus, make it the work of a united front. Ultimately, it is the work of the pope, and as we can only have one pope at a time, it is signed and promulgated by Francis.

What a tremendous example of humility and collaboration is set by both Benedict and Francis in this document. All too often, when someone new comes into a position, for the sake of establishing himself, he sees whatever has been done by his immediate predecessor as no good. The fact that Francis would acknowledge the work done by Benedict and use it to complement his own thought demonstrates that Francis is a pope of humility. The fact that Benedict, the prolific theologian and writer, would permit someone else to put forth his ideas without his name attached to them also shows Benedict as the humble servant leader that he is. Humility and collaboration: two essential ingredients for a good leader, both in the Church and in the world. How blessed we are to have two such examples before us in Pope Francis and Pope

Emeritus Benedict XVI.[37]

Pope Francis's apostolic exhortation *Evangelii Gaudium* ("The Joy of the Gospel," 2013) is a blueprint for all of his work. Theologian Juan Carlos Scannone states that, Pope Francis articulates four priorities that demonstrate his use of the inductive method. The first is "time is more important than space" (*EG* 224), which addresses the importance of patience in the "process of people-building."[38] The second is "unity prevails over conflict" (*EG* 227), which addresses the importance of true dialogue in the creation of a community. The third is "realities are more important than ideas" (*EG* 232), which emphasizes praxis. The fourth is "the whole is greater than the part" (*EG* 234), which seeks to build a world cultural community while still keeping local priorities.

Throughout the document, Pope Francis adopts the method of "look, judge, act" for both ecclesial and societal issues. The first and second chapters of *Evangelii Gaudium* can be viewed as an example of "look" — he examines the nature of the Church and the world and concludes that "a uniform and rigid program of evangelization is not suited to this complex reality" (*EG* 75).[39] The third chapter, "The Proclamation of the Gospel," employs the second step, "judge" — he urges the Church to remember the *sensus fidei* (*EG* 93–97) and states that popular piety must be considered a true *locus fidei* (*EG* 126).[40] The fourth chapter, "The Social Dimension of Evangelization," demonstrates "act" — he calls on Christians, animated by the love of God and the power of the Spirit, to make the Gospel the very center of culture.

With the conclusion of the Second Extraordinary Synod on the Family in 2015 and the subsequent release of his post-synodal exhortation *Amoris Laetitia* ("The Joy of Love," 2016), we see the real beginning of Francis's theological project (which, of course, is a pastoral project as well). Archbishop Charles J. Chaput, OFM Cap, describes *Amoris Laetitia* well: "Papal documents are always important. But — if we can be candid for a moment — some have the energy of a lead brick. *Amoris Laetitia* is very different. It has passages of great wisdom and beauty on marriage and on family life. And it has other passages that have caused some obvious controversy. The controversy has obscured much of the good in the document. So we need to engage the text with open hearts and the discipline of clear thinking." The archbishop goes on to wisely observe:

As a Church we need to meet people where they are. We need to listen to their sufferings and hopes. We need to accompany them along the path of their lives. That demands from us as priests a spirit of patience and mercy. We need to have a bias toward welcoming, and a resistance to seeing individual persons merely as parts of alien or alienated groups. The divorced and civilly remarried are not exiles from Church life. They need to be invited back. The same applies to persons with same-sex attraction. Jesus Christ died for all of us, and we need to behave in a manner that embodies his love.

At the same time, "accompanying" people also means that we need to guide them in the right direction — gently but also honestly, speaking the truth with love. It does no one any good if we "accompany" someone over a cliff, or even worse, to a fatal separation from God. We can't simply confirm people in their mistakes. Scripture is very clear about right and wrong sexual relationships and behavior. We're very poor disciples if we lack the courage to speak the truth as the Church has always understood it.[41]

Continuity, Not Discontinuity

More than anything, I think, when we examine our three most recent popes, we need to avoid the simplistic expression that the first was a philosopher, the second was a theologian, and the third is a pastor. Likewise, we need to avoid the thought of discontinuity. Much as the Second Vatican Council was not a disruption in continuity, there is continuity among all of these pontiffs. What is true for Francis, Benedict, and John Paul, when considering them alongside each other, is true for all the popes, from Saint Peter onward. There has been no rupture, no creation of a "new Church" following the Second Vatican Council (nor has there been the demise of "what was once the Church"). We have the same Church, founded by Jesus Christ. Along the way, there have been some changes in emphasis, but we are still the one, holy, catholic, and apostolic Church.

> **There has been no rupture, no creation of a "new Church" following the Second Vatican Council (nor has there been the demise of "what was once the Church"). We have the same Church, founded by Jesus Christ.**

Points to Remember

- We can learn a great deal about theology by studying the history of theology.
- When we study the history of theology, it is important to remember that God is the central agent in all of the actions.
- There is a greater continuity than any discontinuity in the history of the Church, from Saint Peter, the first pope, up to Francis, our current Holy Father.

Suggestions for Further Reading

For further reading concerning topics in this chapter, you might want to consult the following:

- Blessed Pope Pius IX, *Quanta Cura* (1864)
- Vatican I, *Pastor Aeternus* (1870); *Dei Filius* (1870)
- Pope Leo XIII, *Aeterni Patris* (1879)
- Pope Saint Pius X, *Lamentabili Sane Exitu* (1907); *Pascendi Dominici Gregis* (1907)
- Venerable Pope Pius XII, *Mystici Corporis Christi* (1943); *Divino Afflante Spiritu* (1943); *Mediator Dei* (1947); *Humani Generis* (1950)
- Pope Saint John XXIII, *Humanae Salutis* (1961); *Mater et Magistra*, (1961)
- Vatican II, *Lumen Gentium* (1964); *Gaudium et Spes* (1965); *Dei Verbum* (1965)
- Pope Saint Paul VI, *Populorum Progressio* (1967); *Humanae Vitae* (1968)
- Pope Saint John Paul II, *Pastores Dabo Vobis* (1992); *Veritatis Splendor* (1993); *Fides et Ratio* (1998)
- Joseph Ratzinger/Pope Emeritus Benedict XVI, *Introduction to Christianity* (1968); *The Spirit of the Liturgy* (2000); *Jesus of Nazareth* (2007, 2011, 2012)
- Pope Francis, *Evangelii Gaudium* (2013); *Amoris Laetitia* (2016)

7

How Does the Study of Theology Lead to Holiness of Life?

In this book I contend that the desire to grow in holiness — wanting to be in the presence of God, recognizing who we are in the order of creation, and converting our lives to that end — is at the root of being a good theologian. Holiness leads to good theology, which, in turn, leads to good pastoral practice. There is an old Scholastic axiom, *Nemo dat quod non habet,* which means, "You can't give what you don't have." One aspect of our holistic formation builds on the next. Meaning, if we are striving to be an integral person — one who has a healthy spiritual life (in relation to God, others, and self) and an active intellectual life (rooted in the fonts of Divine Revelation) — then most likely we will desire to transmit the love we have received from the Lord into concrete service of God and neighbor.

If we can say that holiness leads to good theology, does the inverse also ring true? Does good theology lead to holiness? Can study lead to holiness? I contend that it does! Sometimes it is necessary to sacrifice yourself on the altar of your desk. Let's examine these two claims. We will do so in two chapters. This chapter will explore two questions: What does it mean to be holy? What does it mean to have a life of prayer? Our primary guide in this chapter will be the *Catechism of the Catholic Church*. Chapter eight will address the question, What can the wisdom of the saints teach us about good theology leading to holiness of life? Our guides for chapter eight will be a theologian we have mentioned often in this book, Saint Thomas Aquinas, along with a modern theologian, Matthias Joseph Scheeben.

> *Can study lead to holiness? I contend that it does!*
> *Sometimes it is necessary to sacrifice yourself on the*
> *altar of your desk.*

Standing before the Gracious Mystery

What does holiness mean? The bishop who ordained me to the priesthood was Thomas V. Daily. He was a very large man, and I still remember the sheer size of the hands I placed mine in at my priestly ordination. The bishop, a hockey and football player in his youth, enveloped my hands in his and asked if I promised respect and obedience to him and his successors. He then took the oil of chrism and drenched every single inch of my hands, consecrating them and setting them apart for holy things in service of God's holy people. I mention this bishop at the start of this section because, time and again, he would reiterate to us seminarians: "Sometimes holiness is trying to be holy; sometimes the desire for prayer is prayer itself." Holiness begins with the basic knowledge that we are standing before a gracious mystery.

When I was studying for my doctoral degree in Rome at the Pontifical Gregorian University, I was blessed to be assigned as the summer priest at a wonderful parish in my Diocese of Brooklyn, Immaculate Heart of Mary. IHM parish was a great opportunity for me to be the celebrant at Holy Mass daily and to preach to a very diverse community. While I was there, I decided that from June to September, I would focus on the Old Testament. It was a good opportunity for me to pray with the Old Testament, since, naturally enough as a Catholic Christian, my usual *lectio divina* is centered on the Gospels.

So I preached just about every day on the Old Testament reading in the lectionary. Those few months I spent with the people of Israel really gave me a boost spiritually. Books of the Bible that I had studied in seminary, that I had heard proclaimed at the Liturgy of the Hours or in the lectionary of Mass, really came alive. In particular, the First and Second Books of Samuel and the First and Second Books of Kings became steady sources of reflection for me.

The eighth chapter of the First Book of Kings is a remarkable section on which to reflect:

> Solomon stood before the altar of the LORD in the presence of the whole community of Israel, and stretching forth his hands toward heaven, he said, "LORD, God of Israel, there is no God like you in heaven above or on earth below; you keep your covenant of mercy with your servants who are faithful to you with their whole heart.
>
> "Can it indeed be that God dwells on earth? If the heavens and the highest heavens cannot contain you, how much less this temple which I have built! Look kindly on the prayer and petition of your servant, O LORD, my God, and listen to the cry of supplication which I, your servant, utter before you this day. May your eyes watch night and day over this temple, the place where you have decreed you shall be honored; may you heed the prayer which I, your servant, offer in this place. Listen to the petitions of your servant and of your people Israel which they offer in this place. Listen from your heavenly dwell-

ing and grant pardon." (vv. 22–30, NABRE)

Let's compare this Old Testament reading with the Lord's life found in the New Testament. The wisdom of King Solomon recognizes the grandeur and the unknowability of the God present in the Temple. The Lord before whom Solomon offers petition is the *mysterium tremendum et fascinans.*

Rudolf Otto, a German Lutheran theologian, uses this phrase in his book *The Idea of the Holy.*[1] *Mysterium tremendum et fascinans* means "a fearful and fascinating mystery." We can describe the experience that King Solomon undergoes as numinous, meaning something wholly other, something entirely different from what we experience in our everyday lives. It is an experience that is *tremendum*, one that we might best describe as the fear of the Lord. It is an experience that is *fascinans*, one that attracts the believer, because it is merciful, gracious, and loving. The only proper response one can give before such a gracious mystery is that of Solomon — wonder, fear of the Lord, and wholehearted praise. This God of Solomon is a big God, a very big God indeed.

Compare Solomon's encounter with the Divine to Christ's encounter with the Pharisees. In the course of his ministry, Jesus our Lord, who is the Mystery of God Incarnate, experienced the smallness of the God held by the Pharisees and scribes. They — in their smallness of mind and heart — tried to make the God who created them *into their own image.* They fashioned a God who was little, bound by human limitations, and something they could control. Their God is not the God of Abraham, Isaac, and Jacob, not the God who is Jesus Christ, but one who is very small indeed.

Yes, God is God, we are not, and thank God for that! We like to think of ourselves as "self-made" men and women, but ultimately, in the ways that really count, we are not. For no other reason than out of pure love for you and for me, God created us. For no other reason than pure love, God sustains us in being. And for no other reason than pure love, God became a man like us in all things but sin. He suffered and died for us and then, out of pure love, rose again from the dead to give us new and eternal life!

God is not us. But the Father of Mercies deigns to send Mercy himself into the world for us and our salvation. The Holy Spirit, the Paraclete, the bond of love and knowledge that exists from all eternity between the Father and the Son, is shared with us out of the pure graciousness that is the Most Blessed Trinity. How do we have a relationship with God in prayer? How do we grow in holiness, even though we are sinners? Let's turn to the *Catechism* for help!

What Is Prayer?

What is prayer? According to one of the Fathers of the Church, Saint John Damascene, "Prayer is the raising of one's mind and heart to God or the requesting of good things from God" (quoted in CCC 2559). There are four types of prayer: blessing and adoration (recognizing that God is God, we are not, and thank God for that!), contrition (saying we are sorry for our sins and those of the whole world), thanksgiving (showing appreciation to God for everything in our lives, both the happy and the sad), and supplication (pleading to God for our needs and wants and those of others). Let's examine each aspect of prayer in order to see how it relates to growing in holiness. And of course, we will use the *Catechism* as our guide.

> **Prayer is the raising of one's mind and heart to God or the requesting of good things from God.**
> (Saint John Damascene)

Blessing and Adoration

The *Catechism* states: "*Blessing* expresses the basic movement of

Christian prayer: it is an encounter between God and man. In blessing, God's gift and man's acceptance of it are united in dialogue with each other. The prayer of blessing is man's response to God's gifts: because God blesses, the human heart can in return bless the One who is the source of every blessing" (CCC 2626). Adoration is described as "the first attitude of man acknowledging that he is a creature before his creator" (CCC 2628). Note what the *Catechism* is telling us: It is all about two *r*s needed for the spiritual life: religion and relationship.

At its essence, what is religion? We could say that it is the human being's response to God as God reveals himself to human beings. This is a very simple way of saying that it is a relationship or, to use a biblical word, a covenant. It is a relationship between two unequal partners. God, the faithful partner, is always the one who initiates the relationship. The human being, perpetually falling into unfaithfulness, is the one who responds to this covenantal offer from God with true and proper worship of God. Man realizes that he is completely, totally dependent on God. And that's okay!

Contrition

One summer when I was a seminarian, I was blessed to be assigned to a pastoral internship at a small parish in England. I am an Anglophile, so it was a true pleasure to experience life in an area outside of Oxford. The thrill of going to The Eagle and Child (the pub where the "Inklings" — a group of writers that included J. R. R. Tolkien and C. S. Lewis — would meet to have a pint) and entering the same churches where Saint John Henry Newman preached was altogether too much for me. I loved it!

What I especially loved was the parish life — observing a parish priest who loved his people dearly, who gave them the best possible homilies and liturgy, as well as his own fatherly presence. I also loved visiting the parish school, which was in session up to the middle of July.

One of the tasks that I was given as a young seminarian was to work with the schoolchildren. On my first day there, one of the catechists said to me: "Whatever you do, please do not mention the *s* word to the children." I struggled to think of what words beginning with *s* I should not mention in front of the children — and was then informed that the *s* word was "sin" and that I should not mention it because it makes people feel bad. If sin makes people feel bad, that's a good thing, because sin is a bad thing indeed!

In the eleventh chapter of Saint John's Gospel, the Lord Jesus calls Lazarus out of the tomb. We read that Lazarus comes out, bound hand and foot, and the Lord says these simple words: "Unbind him, and let him go" (Jn 11:44). The Lord Jesus is saying those same words to us right now. What's binding us up and refusing to let us go? I'd venture to guess it is sin. This affords us the opportunity to reflect upon exactly what sin is.

In the Book of Genesis, we learn the story of our first parents, Adam and Eve, and their fall from their primordial state of original innocence. As the *Catechism* reminds us, the Church's doctrine of original sin is "the reverse side of the Good News" (CCC 389). The ultimate truth is the Good News of our faith: Salvation comes in and through Christ Jesus our Lord. As the *Catechism* reminds us: "The Church, which has the mind of Christ, knows very well that we cannot tamper with the revelation of original sin without undermining the mystery of Christ" (CCC 389).

What Exactly Is Sin?

Let's take a few moments to clarify what we mean by sin before we look to the Good News of the Gospel to learn a remedy for sin. First, we have to start with original sin. So what exactly is original sin? We read in the *Catechism* that original sin is, ultimately, lack of trust in the Creator and abuse of the great gift of free will given to us from God our Father (CCC 397).

In the sin of choosing to disobey the one thing that the Creator had asked our first parents to do — namely, to refrain from eating of the fruit of the tree of the knowledge of good and evil — Adam and Eve forgot their place in the universe. They forgot that God is Creator and that they were creatures. They who were called to be "like God" suddenly decided that they wanted to be "without God, before God and not in accordance with God" (CCC 398). They who were created in the image and likeness of God began to reflect a distorted likeness (CCC 400), almost like the images in a funhouse mirror. Everything was put into disarray, and all their relationships were thrown asunder.

Threefold Alienation

In human relationships, the human being is divided. In himself and in his thoughts, he is torn between two things. He knows in the deepest part of his soul that he is created to know, serve, and love God in this life and to be with him in the next. But if he's honest, he also knows he really wants to serve himself first. His focus is on the things of this world, not on his true home, heaven. The human being's relationship with the world is — due to original sin — disordered.

As the *Catechism* reminds us, "visible creation has become alien and hostile to man," and relationships with fellow humans have become difficult. Even the most primordial relationship, that of man and woman, is "subject to tensions, their relations henceforth marked by lust and domination" (CCC 400). We see the bad fruits of sin: a threefold alienation of the human being from God, others, and self. And we see the true wages of sin: death.

We learn that this original sin leads to personal sin. Oftentimes, people seem to be unclear as to a definition of what is a sin and what isn't a sin. It's actually quite simple. Again, we can turn to the *Catechism* to glean a clearer understanding: "Sin is an offense against reason, truth, and right conscience; it is failure in genuine love for God and neighbor caused by a perverse attachment to certain goods. It wounds the nature of man and injures human solidarity. It has been defined as 'an utterance, a deed, or a desire contrary to the eternal law'" (CCC 1849).

We know there are two types of sin: mortal sin, which destroys charity in our hearts and turns us away from the love that is God himself, and venial sin, which permits charity — that fundamental aspect of our spiritual life — to exist in a lesser, weakened, and wounded form in our hearts (CCC 1855).

What, then, constitutes a sin? Basically, mortal sin requires three things: grave matter, full knowledge, and complete consent (CCC 1857–1860). To sin, we have to know that what we're doing is wrong and freely choose to do it anyway. Sin can be something that we do (sins of commission) or something we fail to do (sins of omission).[2]

Sin is the flip side of the Good News. But we must focus not on the sickness of sin but on the cure for the illness — namely, repentance and holiness of life. And the only one who can cure us is the Divine Physician — Jesus our Lord.

Threefold Reconciliation

At its root, sin is a threefold alienation from God, others, and our own selves. What we need, then, to battle this alienation is a threefold reconciliation that can only come from one who is like us in all things but sin — and who is also fully divine. It can only come in and through the Lord Jesus, true man and true God.

> *At its root, sin is a threefold alienation from God, others, and our own selves. What we need, then, to battle this alienation is a threefold reconciliation that can only come from one who is like us in all things but sin — and who is also fully divine.*

Our lack of basic integrity has to be healed. Jesus opens his arms wide on the cross in an embrace of love for you and me. Through his action of total self-giving, he conquers sin and death to bring us to new life. How can we become whole? How can we learn to be healed by the Lord Jesus, who wishes nothing more than to heal and save us? It is simple. The Church gives us three traditional ways: prayer, fasting, and almsgiving.

Prayer gets us in touch with the Lord; it helps us to become more aware of the deepest desires of our human hearts through the cultivation of an open, receptive, and listening attitude. Fasting — denying ourselves the pleasures of the body — reminds us that our true home lies not here but in heaven. It teaches us the great virtue of temperance, so needed today in our world of excess. Almsgiving makes us aware that the time during which we are placed on this earth is not about ourselves — that it is never about ourselves; it is always about the Lord and always about others. Consider the first two commandments: Love the Lord your God with all your heart, soul, and mind. Love your neighbor as yourself.

The Necessity of the Sacrament of Penance

The surest way to obtain healing is through the Sacrament of Penance. It is the cure for the sickness that is sin. As the *Catechism of the Catholic Church* tells us, it is sin that ruptures our communion with God and the Church (1440). It is the Lord alone who forgives sins so that we might have the possibility to change our lives, to convert, and to recover the grace of justification (1446). The penitent needs to have contrition and sorrow for his or her sins, confess them, and do the penance assigned.

Never be afraid of the Sacrament of Penance. Nothing should keep us from this sacrament. Perhaps it has been many years since you have been to confession. Perhaps you don't remember the Rite of Penance or have forgotten how to say an Act of Contrition. This should not hold you back from receiving the love and mercy that the Lord Jesus has for you.

Basic Questions about Penance

The two basic questions I'm asked regarding the Sacrament of Penance are these: First, why do I have to tell my sins to a priest? Second, why do I have to say my sins aloud? First, we go to a priest because he is the minister of the reconciliation that Jesus wishes to give to us. Yes, the priest is a sinner — everyone is. He, too, needs to seek out the Sacrament of Penance often, as we all should. I believe that in order to be a good confessor, a priest must be a good and regular penitent himself. When we go to confession, we are going to Christ. The priest, by virtue of his ordination (and not because of his own worthiness), stands *in persona Christi*, in the Person of Christ. He stands as Christ, the Good Shepherd; as Christ, the Good Samaritan; as Christ, the long-patient father of the prodigal son (CCC 1465). In this sacramental moment, the priest stands as the human face of the mercy that is Jesus. Do not be afraid to tell him anything you need to say. He will not be shocked, and he will not think less of you. The seal of the Sacrament of Penance is present, and he will never violate its absolute sacred secrecy.

Second, yes, the Lord knows our sins already; he knows all things. But when we say our sins aloud in the privacy of the confessional, we acknowledge what we have done and what we have failed to do. We own up to our faults and — having owned up to them — we take the first step toward healing them. On this topic, Pope Benedict XVI (as Joseph Cardinal Ratzinger) wrote: "Of course, the confession of one's own sin can seem to be something heavy for the person, because it humbles his pride and confronts him with his poverty. It is this that we need: we suffer exactly for this reason: we shut ourselves up in our delirium of guiltlessness and for this reason we are closed to others and to any comparison with them."[3]

The Church is clear in the path that she lays out for us to follow. We need to become aware of our sins, and having owned up to them, we need not to despair but to trust in the Lord who desires nothing more than to heal and save us. May the prayer of the psalmist be ours: "Let your mercy, O LORD, be upon us, / even as we hope in you" (Ps 33:22).

Thanksgiving

The *Catechism* gives us two terse paragraphs on the prayer of thanksgiving. They read:

> Thanksgiving characterizes the prayer of the Church which, in celebrating the Eucharist, reveals and becomes more fully what she is. Indeed, in the work of salvation, Christ sets creation free from sin and death to consecrate it anew and make it return to the Father, for his glory. The thanksgiving of the members of the Body participates in that of their Head.
>
> As in the prayer of petition, every event and need can become an offering of thanksgiving. The letters of St. Paul often begin and end with thanksgiving, and the Lord Jesus is always present in it: "Give thanks in all circumstances; for this is the will of God in Christ Jesus for you"; "Continue steadfastly in prayer, being watchful in it with thanksgiving." (2637–2638)

Note the wisdom of the *Catechism*: the prayer of thanksgiving is intrinsically tied to the Holy Eucharist. The key to holiness is indeed the Eucharist, the true presence of Christ. Let's examine, through the Gospel of Saint John, exactly what we as Catholics believe about the Eucharist.

The Bread of Life Discourse is found in the sixth chapter of John. John's Gospel is so different from the other Gospels that some Scripture scholars have nicknamed it the "Maverick Gospel."[4] This Gospel begins in the high realms of space, time, and eternity and then quickly goes right to Jesus' baptism by John in the River Jordan.

"Unless You Eat My Flesh ... "

John's Gospel is not different from the others just in style and tone. True to its nickname of being the "Maverick Gospel," it offers some unusual content. In the middle of the first part of John's Gospel, Jesus gives an extended talk to the crowd. He stands before them and says: "Unless you eat the flesh of the Son of man and drink his blood, you have no life in you" (Jn 6:53). And as is the way with human nature when confronted with God and the things of God, some of those present hear his words and embrace him, whereas others reject him. Some decide what he's saying is altogether too much for them.

Imagine for a moment that you are in the crowd. You have never heard this man Jesus speak, but you have come out to hear him because of all the signs he has been performing. Perhaps, you think, he might perform a sign today, and you might be amazed. And here he is in front of you, the great teacher, the one some say might be the long-awaited Messiah. When he speaks, it is to say things which others will describe as "difficult things."

Difficult things, indeed! "Eat my flesh, drink my blood if you wish to have my life in you." What is he talking about? Is he speaking metaphorically? Surely, he doesn't mean all of this literally, does he? What does he mean by "life"?

As we will come to realize, the Lord Jesus is not simply speaking symbolically. He's not just using a figure of speech, an extended metaphor. What he is speaking of is the gift of the Eucharist, his true Body, his true Blood, poured out for you and me, for us and for our salvation.

These words of the Word of Life himself cause all who hear them to take a pause and reflect on what he is saying. When Jesus speaks of his Body and his Blood in this passage of Scripture, he is not speaking in metaphors or through hyperbole or even describing the situation analogously. No, he means what he says, and he says what he means. The Eucharist, which we celebrate day after day on the altars of all the world's Catholic churches and chapels, the Eucharist that is adored in all the tabernacles of the world, is his true Body and his true Blood.

Notions about the Eucharist

In 2019, the Pew Research Center released the results of a survey[5] containing the following startling statistics: "In fact, nearly seven-in-ten Catholics (69%) say they personally believe that during Catholic Mass, the bread and wine used in Communion 'are *symbols* of the body and blood of Jesus Christ.' Just one-third of U.S. Catholics (31%) say they believe that 'during Catholic Mass, the bread and wine actually become the body and blood of Jesus.'"[6] Bishop Robert Barron, a great modern Roman Catholic writer and dialoguer with contemporary culture, was, naturally enough, upset and discouraged by this information. In response, he enlisted his Word on Fire Catholic Ministries to prepare catechetical material,[7] as well as releasing a video response himself.[8]

These are shockingly low numbers of people who seem to understand the Church's teaching on the Eucharist! What does the Church teach concerning the Real Presence of Christ in the Eucharist? Our primary source for this examination will be the *Catechism of the Catholic Church* (part two, section two, chapter two, article three, paragraphs 1322–1419). We, as Catholics, believe that during the Mass — with the invocation of the Holy Spirit and the words of consecration, at the hands of a validly ordained priest — the bread and wine are truly and substantially (meaning at their core, at their truest, deepest meanings) changed into the Body and Blood of our Lord and Savior, Jesus Christ.

It is not a mere symbol. Jesus Christ himself is truly, substantially present in the Eucharistic species; his Body and his Blood, his soul and divinity, are given to us so that we might share in the new and eternal life given to us. This concept is affirmed not only in the *Catechism* but also in the Council of Trent. We call this the doctrine of transubstantiation.

> *Jesus Christ himself is truly, substantially present in the Eucharistic species; his Body and his Blood, his soul and divinity, are given to us so that we might share in the new and eternal life given to us.*

The Mass

We, as Catholics, share in the Bread of Life that Jesus describes in this sixth chapter of John's Gospel. Every Eucharistic celebration is a participation in the Last Supper of the Lord. Every Eucharistic celebration is a participation in Christ's sacrifice on Calvary. Every Eucharistic celebration is a participation in the resurrection of Jesus Christ from the dead. This is what we call the paschal mystery of the Lord.

The Eucharist, in which we are made one body in Christ, is "the heart and the summit of the Church's life" (CCC 1407). The Church makes the Eucharist, and the Eucharist, in turn, makes the Church. It is the "source and summit" (*Lumen Gentium*, 11) of the life of the Church. It is the most important and the highest worship we can give to God.

At the Mass, time and eternity meet. Heaven and earth kiss. God and humankind are made one in the one, true sacrifice of Christ. The *Catechism of the Catholic Church* reminds us: "As sacrifice, the Eucharist is also offered in reparation for the sins of the living and the dead and to obtain spiritual or temporal benefits from God" (1414).

In reality, the question as it is often posed to Catholics — "What is the Eucharist?" — is not valid. The interrogative pronoun used is wrong. The question should be "Who is the Eucharist?" What do I mean by using "Who" rather than "What"? The Eucharist is not a thing. It is not a commodity or an object to "have." It is the sacramental presence of the Lord Jesus Christ. Yes, the Eucharist, whose very name means "thanksgiving," is something for which we should be thanking God daily. His true and Real Presence is a gift. The Eucharist, simply put, is Jesus. It is gift and mystery.

Saint Thomas Aquinas and the Eucharist

One of the great saints of our Church, the Angelic Doctor, Saint Thomas Aquinas, offers us an immense and unique contribution to the Catholic understanding of the Eucharist. Bishop Robert Barron wrote a book many years ago on Saint Thomas titled *Thomas Aquinas: Spiritual Master* (Crossroad, 1997). I read it while I was a seminarian, and it had a profound impact on my own thinking about theology, spirituality, and the Eucharist.

One main point runs throughout Bishop Barron's text: Far from being a dry and dusty old philosopher who created obscure doctrines that are difficult to understand, Saint Thomas was a man in love with Jesus Christ. All the theology that he wrote, all the philosophy that he helped to clarify, were a deep and beautiful labor of love for Saint Thomas. For him, there was no distinction between philosophy and theology, between dogma and spirituality, between our prayer lives and our "real" lives. All was one, and Thomas, ultimately a scriptural theologian, was truly, deeply enraptured with the one Divine Person with two natures, human and divine, the one who is fully God and fully human, Jesus Christ our Lord.

Jesus was the center of Saint Thomas's life. The *Doctor Communis*, the universal Doctor of the Church, had a tremendous mystical experience on December 6, 1273, the feast of Saint Nicholas. While writing about the Eucharist — in fact, he was studying and trying his best to offer a synthesis on all the Church's teachings on the Eucharist — he had a vision in which the corpus, the figure of Christ on a crucifix, spoke to him. Our Lord said to him, *"Bene scripsisti de me, Thoma. Quam ergo mercedem accipies"* ("You have written well of me, Thomas. Whatever you desire, I will grant you").

What Would **You** Say?

Imagine that our Lord Jesus spoke directly to you. Imagine, just for a moment, that he said to you that whatever you most wanted in life, he would give you. What would you say? What would I say? Putting aside for a moment all the things I think I would say, what would I *really* say? Would I ask for power, for prestige, for material goods, for blessings on my family and friends? For what would I ask? What would you say?

Well, Thomas looked at his Lord with love and said four little words: *"Nil nisi te, Domine."* What does that mean? Quite simply, "Nothing but you, Lord." Why? Why would he say that? Why would he say that when he could have asked for so many other things — good things, practical things, things that would help make the world a better place, things that could make his life happier? I believe that Saint Thomas responded this way because he knew, above all else, that if you have the Lord Jesus, you have everything. When we have the Eucharist, we have Jesus, truly, substantially present under the form of the consecrated bread and wine.

Not simply a sign, not merely a symbol, the Eucharist whom we celebrate each and every day in Masses all over the world — and Sunday after Sunday as a people gathered together — is Our Lord, just as he himself promises to us in the Bread of Life Discourse. Jesus tells us in the Gospel of John 6:53–55: "Amen, amen, I say to you, unless you eat the flesh of the Son of Man and drink his blood, you do not have life within you. Whoever eats my flesh and drinks my blood has eternal life, and I will raise him on the last day" (NABRE).

He tells us that he himself is the Bread of Life. He is the Bread of Life on which we feast. It is the Lord Jesus himself who lives in us, so that we become living tabernacles of Christ, the most high God, when we receive him. Saint Thomas tells us: "The things that we love tell us what we are." Do we love Jesus Christ in the Eucharist with our whole hearts and souls? Do we try our best to learn the Church's doctrines about the Eucharist and then communicate them to the world? This is the task and challenge given to us in the Bread of Life Discourse.

Forming a Eucharistic Spirituality

How, practically speaking, might we best form a Eucharistic spirituality, primarily focused on the Mass? The following tips are meant to be helpful and are in no way meant to exclude any other spiritualities or devotions to the Eucharist. They are simply things that I've personally found helpful as a priest, a spiritual director, and, above all, as a Catholic Christian believer.

The Importance of Holy Mass

I propose that we need to see the Mass as the single most important thing in our day. Nothing in our spiritual lives as Catholic Christians is as important as the Mass because the Mass brings us Jesus' Real Presence in the Eucharist. The Mass is the central action of the Church's life. On the altar heaven and earth meet, time and eternity kiss, and God and humankind are reconciled. The Mass is, above all else, the celebration of the paschal mystery of the Church — Christ has died, Christ is risen, Christ will come again!

> *Nothing in our spiritual lives as Catholic Christians is as important as the Mass because the Mass brings us Jesus' Real Presence in the Eucharist.*

I began to appreciate the Mass during my time as a high school student. Mass was part of each day, and I was invited by the wonderful priests who served on the faculty to become more involved in the liturgy as a sacristan. This experience was a pivotal and integral part of my awareness of my own priestly vocation. The priests on the faculty at that time were diverse. They had totally different personalities and interests, taught different subjects, and moderated all sorts of different activities — but the things that united these good men who became my personal role models and heroes were their sharing in the ordained priesthood of Jesus Christ and their obvious love, care, and devotion to the daily celebration of the Mass. To this day, I thank God for my time at this school as a student and, many years later, as a priest on the faculty there. It made me fall in love with the Eucharist.

By getting involved in the Eucharistic celebration, by learning about the Mass, by serving as a sacristan of the chapel and as an altar server, I felt a sense of ownership and responsibility in the Mass. All of us, no matter the vocation with which we have been blessed, have an active and full part to play in the celebration of the Mass.

Get involved! Volunteer in a parish liturgical ministry in which you feel comfortable. All ministries are valued, all are needed, all help Christ to build up the Kingdom of God right here, right now. As the Second Vatican Council's *Sacrosanctum Concilium* (Constitution on the Sacred Liturgy) teaches us, the liturgy is enriched by our full, conscious, and active participation.

Preparing for Mass

We might wish to prepare ourselves before the celebration of the liturgy by gaining a familiarity with the readings that will be proclaimed during the Mass. By reading them before Mass, we prepare ourselves to hear them proclaimed at Mass with a clear mind and heart, and we allow the liturgy to be that much richer.

We also might arrive a few moments prior to the start of Mass in order to fully recollect ourselves, to form an intention in our minds and hearts, so that we each, in our own ways, as ordained and lay, might help make real the sacrifice of the Mass. By prayerful recollection and by making an act of thanksgiving after receiving Holy Communion, we allow ourselves to realize exactly who is living inside of us at that moment — Jesus Christ our Lord.

We can become him whom we have received. In our baptisms, we become one with Christ. We form the Body of Christ, with the Lord as the head and us as the members. We can begin to appreciate the grace that comes to us in and through the Eucharistic mystery. Remember, all of the sacraments give us God's grace, that totally free and undeserved gift of God's life in us, but only the Eucharist gives us God himself, Jesus Christ, the Lord.

Saint Thomas once wrote: "Three things are necessary for the salvation of man: to know what he ought to believe; to know what he ought to desire; and to know what he ought to do." May we always appreciate and know the doctrine of Jesus in the Eucharist, may we always desire Jesus in the Eucharist, and may we always celebrate the Eucharist worthily and well.

> *For a Christian, every moment of our lives has to become a moment of thanksgiving.*

All Is Grace?

With a proper understanding of the Eucharist, the font of holiness and life, we can then turn to the second part of what the *Catechism* teaches us about thanksgiving. It's easy to believe in God when everything is going great; it's easy to praise the Lord when everything in our lives seems to be in order. It gets a lot tougher when everything seems to be going wrong! Yet for a Christian, every moment of our lives has to become a moment of thanksgiving.

Every moment of our lives, every single person whom we meet, every smile and every tear, is a gift from God. All of it helps to shape us into the persons we are called to be. Like the dying abbé in Georges Bernanos's famous novel *The Diary of a Country Priest*, we can say, *"Tout est grâce"* ("All is grace").[9] Everything depends upon how we cooperate with the grace of God pouring down freely upon us in our lives.

Then What Is Grace?
We might ask ourselves, then: "What is grace?" The *Catechism* offers us a great explanation. It beautifully reads:

> Our justification comes from the grace of God. Grace is *favor*, the *free* and *undeserved help* that God gives us to respond to his call to become children of God, adoptive sons, partakers of the divine nature and of eternal life.
>
> Grace is a *participation in the life of God*. It introduces us into the intimacy of Trinitarian life: by Baptism the Christian participates in the grace of Christ, the Head of his Body. As an "adopted son" he can henceforth call God "Father," in union with the only Son. He receives the life of the Spirit who breathes charity into him and who forms the Church.
>
> This vocation to eternal life is *supernatural*. It depends entirely on God's gratuitous initiative, for he alone can reveal and give himself. It surpasses the power of human intellect and will, as that of every other creature. (1996–1998)

As we stated earlier, God offers grace, but we have to accept it! We have to be open and attentive to it! Every moment of our lives is an opportunity either to grow in grace or to fall into sin; every moment of our lives is a chance to practice either virtue or vice.

Supplication

A great deal of our time in prayer is spent praying for our needs and the needs of others. Did you ever try to cut deals with God in prayer? Did you ever say to God, "Lord, if I give this up (or if I do, or don't do, this thing), then you should grant me this"? It's like God is a genie in a bottle with whom we can bargain. This never ends well!

The Model Is Mary

The mature Christian is able to go before the Lord in true supplication. What does this type of prayer look like? The model for this, as in all things, comes from our Blessed Mother, Mary. Early on in John's Gospel (2:1–12), Our Lord, his Mother, and his disciples are invited to a wedding feast in Cana in Galilee. We read that wine for the guests at this wedding runs out and that, so there will be no embarrassment for the newly married couple, the Mother of God brings this situation to her Son's attention. The Lord, knowing that this wedding is perhaps not the most opportune time for him to perform the first of his signs, all of which will point to the fact that he is the Messiah, simply asks her: "Woman, how does your concern affect me? My hour has not yet come" (Jn 2:4, NABRE).

Mary, Our Lady, our dear precious Mother, simply draws the situation to the attention of her Beloved Son. That's all she needs to do. And then our Mother gives the best advice that she can give to anyone: "Do whatever he tells you" (Jn 2:5). And it is this request, coming from the heart of his Mother, our Mother of Mercy, that leads the Lord to perform the first of his signs.

That's the way it is. We need to turn to our Mother, who loves us and always pleads for us as advocate and intercessor. She brings our cares to the Lord, and he answers according to his gracious will.

A healthy devotion to the Mother of God is a quality that I

look for in the seminarians I am blessed to form. There are many signs of a Catholic gentleman, but an important one — almost more than any other — is having a rosary in his pocket (and not just having it but praying it). Mary is our Mother. As we respect and honor our own mothers who have given us life, so too we honor our Mother, the Mother of Mercy.

The Mother of Mercy

One of the best images of Mary as Mother of Mercy, in my opinion, comes from a prayer card commemorating a dear friend's perpetual profession of vows as a Religious Sister of Mercy of Alma, Michigan. The image is striking. It was painted by this sister's biological sister, a talented professional artist. In it, Our Lady raises up a chalice, and light — the Light of Christ — pours into it. Our Mother of Mercy, she who brings forth the Light of the World into this world of darkness is, at the same time, both active and contemplative. She holds up her arms, grasping the chalice, boldly raising that natural cup up for its supernatural purpose. At the same time, Our Mother of Mercy is demure, receptive, and humble, not gazing upwards to the beauty descending down, but allowing herself to become incorporated into the Eternal Mystery of the All-Beautiful One. In doing so, she becomes even more strikingly beautiful. It is precisely in being demure, precisely in being humble, precisely in being obedient, that Mary is Queen. The natural nobility she bears, coming from her Immaculate Conception and birth, forged in the crucible of her suffering and sorrows, demonstrates that she is Queen and Mother.

Through our Queen and Mother, Mary, our ignoble nature finds its noble source and summit. We find our source in prayer — deep, solid prayer that incorporates the liturgical and devotional, and encourages growth in the desire for quiet reflection. A Religious Sister of Mercy of Alma, Michigan, who helps form young sisters told me that the novice should develop a longing to spend time spontaneously in the chapel, to recharge with the One whom she loves. This is such a Marian statement. I am convinced that the world will be saved not through frenetic activity but through the sacrifice of devotional and contemplative prayer, and especially through the Eucharist.

> *The world will be saved not through frenetic activity, but through the sacrifice of devotional and contemplative prayer, and especially through the Eucharist.*

Mary knows in her heart of hearts and in her soul of souls that this fierce, all-too-human struggle between good and evil that her beloved Son experiences on this earthly plane is for the salvation of the world. Every cut he receives, every bruise he endures, every insult and calumny he hears, every indignity of every bit of spittle he suffers — none of it, none of it is in vain. She knows in her heart of hearts and in her soul of souls that what her beloved Son, the only Son of a widowed Mother, endures on this earthly plane leads to a supernatural level in which Satan is roundly defeated, and the prince of lies is made subject to the One who is All Truth.

Our Mother of Mercy knows this truth not only through the direct experience of being with her Son, Our Lord, but also through contemplation. Imagine Mary engaging in the first form of adoration, holding her child, this remarkable little project accomplished by the Lord and herself, through the power of the Holy Spirit.

Mary, our Mother, has one thing that we must possess now more than ever, and that is *hope*. Hope is precisely what we need today. Our Lady knows that the Lord has pity on us. She knows the love that pours forth from his Sacred Heart, which beats in a pure rhythm of love for us. She has the confident assurance that he is the ultimate victor over every trial, every adversity. That's what makes her the Mercy of God in the midst of the misery of mankind.

Knowing the Difference between Our Wants and Our Needs

A true understanding of supplication requires us to be mature enough to know the differences between our wants and our needs. We might think of it this way: God answers all of our needs, not all of our wants. Sacred Scripture tells us: "You open your hand, you satisfy the desire of every living thing" (Ps 145).

If I were granted all of my wants throughout my life — all of the things that, in my sins and in my cognitive distortions, I thought I wanted — would those things really be what I needed? Absolutely not! Everything happens for a purpose, even difficult things that aren't included in the list of things we think we want. Everything can work toward growth in life — and, by our participating in God's will for us, everything can work to bring us toward the eternal life to come. "What does it matter? All is grace!"

The Key to Holiness

In the Gospel of Mark, Our Lord is continuing his ministry of healing and teaching when he encounters Bartimaeus, the blind son of Timaeus (10:46–52). Saint Mark explains that Bartimaeus has been sitting on the side of the road leading out of Jericho. Bartimaeus cannot see. He is left behind by so many who pass him by without giving him a second thought.

And yet somehow, Bartimaeus hears about Jesus. He learns of the mighty signs and wonders that this man from Nazareth, a wise rabbi without peer, has performed. Bartimaeus knows that this Jesus, somehow, can heal him. He knows that this Jesus is somehow the long-awaited Holy One of God.

When Jesus passes by, Bartimaeus sits on the side of the road, no doubt overshadowed by the crowd that has turned out to see Jesus. He wants Jesus. Bartimaeus cries out for him, to him. And he is shushed, quieted, rebuked by the crowd, told to be silent. However, Bartimaeus cries out all the more, louder and louder, until the Master hears him. The wise and gentle Jesus hears him and stops, bidding him to come forward to him. Because of his persistence, because of his faith, Bartimaeus is healed and cured.

What can we learn from the example of blind Bartimaeus for growth in our prayer lives? Simply this: Be persistent! We don't give up, even when it may seem that we are getting no results.

Sometimes when we pray, we are filled with great consolation. We can feel God's presence. Other times, we feel nothing; it's as though we're simply going through the motions. But never forget that, even in the silence, in the desolation, God is there. He is with us. He is listening. God answers all of our prayers, but sometimes the answer is "no." Sometimes what we think we want is not what's best for us or others. God answers all of our prayers, but sometimes the answer is "not yet." God, who hears all of our prayers, answers in his own time, not in ours. The key is to be like Bartimaeus — even when we cannot see, we keep on crying out. Don't give up. Jesus is passing by, a hundred times a day. Just keep on crying out; the Lord is listening!

Points to Remember

- Holiness of life leads to good theology. Therefore, the one who wishes to be a good theologian must grow in holiness. ("*Nemo dat quod non habet*" — "You can't give what you don't have.")
- Prayer is essential for holiness. Holiness begins with trying to be holy.
- "Prayer is the raising of one's mind and heart to God or requesting good things from God" (Saint John Damascene).
- The prayer of adoration comes from recognizing

who we are in right relationship to God, the Creator.
Remember, God is God, we are not, and thank God
for that!

- The prayer of contrition comes from knowing that
we are all sinners, redeemed and forgiven by God.
The Sacrament of Penance is our great aid for growth
in true holiness.
- The prayer of thanksgiving comes from the highest
form of thanksgiving — the Eucharist. The Christian growing in maturity is able to recognize the
movements of grace in life.
- The prayer of supplication has our Mother of Mercy,
Mary, as the model. The mature Christian, striving
to grow in holiness, is able to distinguish wants from
needs. Ultimately, God answers all of our needs, but
not necessarily all of our wants.
- Growth in prayer can only come from persistence.

8

Toward a Spirituality of Study

I f you ask my sister-in-law, who has known me since I was eight years old, she will tell you that she always remembers me with a book in my hand. And it's true: Guilty as charged, I love reading! My sister, who has spent her life as a Catholic school teacher, was ten years older than I, and as a precocious, budding teacher, she decided that it was high time for me to learn to read at the age of three. I have never looked back!

It started with comic books — a pleasure that this confirmed nerd still has (with a particular affection for the Hulk from Marvel and Batman from DC) — and then moved into detective novels, such as Sherlock Holmes, the Choose Your Own Adventure series (along with its poor country cousin, the Find Your Fate series), all of which eventually led to a love of Ray Bradbury, copies of *Alfred Hitchcock Mystery Magazines*, Stephen King, and Michael Crichton.

By college age, even as a seminarian, I knew that I wanted to double major in philosophy (which was necessary and required) and English. It was at this time that I fell in love with T. S. Eliot, Shakespeare, Goethe, Dante, Flannery O'Connor, Graham

Greene, and Walker Percy. (You'll find my suggestions for the creation of a reading list in both classics and Catholic literature in the appendixes of this book.)

My love of reading has translated into a love of study. Studying is a huge part of my life and my own spirituality. The Lord has given us the opportunity to learn. As we have discussed in this book, theology is learning about someone whom we love and whom we desire to know even more intimately — our Lord Jesus. So how can a Catholic develop a spirituality of studying?

Wisdom — "Be Attentive!"

Earlier on, in chapter five, we explored the theological method of Saint Thomas Aquinas. In what is considered to be his greatest work, the *Summa Theologiae*, Saint Thomas tackles what he believes is the true object of *Sacra Doctrina*. He writes: "This doctrine [theology] is wisdom above all human wisdom; not merely in any one order, but absolutely" (*ST*, I, q.1, a.6). According to Saint Thomas, one needs to be truly wise to study theology. It is the study of the highest things; ultimately, it is the study of God. Therefore, if one is studying the highest things (and judging these highest things as well) and is not wise, he or she will be like the man in Matthew 7:24–27 who builds his house on sand. All that he is trying to construct will collapse without the firm foundation that is wisdom.

A wise theologian studies the highest cause, God, most properly by placing the lower studies — subjects that are absolutely necessary for understanding, such as philosophy — in the proper order. Thus, the wise theologian will have the requisite firm foundation. I began to understand this so much more clearly one year when I was teaching a seminar on theological method. My students and I had numerous discussions on how poor philosophy leads to poor theology and how holiness of life leads to good theology. One of my students, just a first-year theologian, wrote a brilliant paper on the topic of holiness of life leading to good theology and vice versa, using Saint Thomas as the model — and I am indebted to him for teaching me!

Two Types of Wisdom

In the *Summa Theologiae*, Saint Thomas distinguishes the true meaning of wisdom. He states:

> Since judgment appertains to wisdom, the twofold manner of judging produces a twofold wisdom. A man may judge in one way by inclination, as whoever has the habit of a virtue judges rightly of what concerns that virtue by his very inclination toward it. Hence it is the virtuous man, as we read, who is the measure and rule of human acts. In another way, by knowledge, just as a man learned in moral science might be able to judge rightly about virtuous acts, though he had not the virtue. The first manner of judging divine things belongs to that wisdom which is set down among the gifts of the Holy Ghost: "The spiritual man judgeth all things" (1 Cor. 2:15). And Dionysius says (Div. Nom. ii): "Hierotheus is taught not by mere learning, but by experience of divine things." The second manner of judging belongs to this doctrine which is acquired by study, though its principles are obtained by revelation. (I, q.1, a.6)

The Angelic Doctor believes there are two ways of judging, one based on knowledge and the other on habit. The first type is based on knowledge and learning — for instance, one can learn all about Christian dogma and morals. It's possible, however, to learn these things intellectually but never truly integrate virtue into one's life. One could know how to describe what faith, hope, and charity are without truly possessing these theological virtues. This type of wisdom can only go so far. You can study about the things that compose holiness but never permit yourself to become holy.

The second type of judging arises from a habit of virtue, which in turn leads to right judgment. If a person allows him- or herself to embrace wisdom, then he or she can judge rightly the things of God. This wisdom of which Saint Thomas writes comes not from reason but as a gift from the Holy Spirit — and, as such, it can only be obtained by one who is in a state of grace and who is striving for genuine holiness. Wisdom and holiness of life are the true mark of a theologian.

> **Wisdom and holiness of life are the true mark of a theologian.**

Holiness leads to good theology. Filled with this gift of the Holy Spirit and the gift of true wisdom, a theologian is a man or woman of faith. He or she, armed with the human learning acquired from years of studying and learning, and fortified by the habit of the virtue of wisdom, is thus capable of truly being a theologian. The twentieth-century Canadian theologian Bernard Lonergan describes the following as the "transcendental precepts": Be attentive! Be intelligent! Be reasonable! Be responsible! Be open and receptive to the guidance of the Holy Spirit![1]

Good Theology Leads to Holiness

Let's examine someone whose theology has stood the test of time. There are certain theologians whom even those who are just beginning their studies know, such as Saints Augustine, Anselm, and Thomas Aquinas. There are others whom students of theology get to know, at least by name, pretty quickly, such as Joseph Ratzinger and Hans Urs von Balthasar. And then there are those whom you discover years and years later, those who have influenced some great theologians you've studied and whose theology you have adapted into your own understanding of the world. They are the theologians you kind of heard about in passing but never read. Then, when you do finally get around to reading them, you realize how great they are. One such theologian for me is Matthias Joseph Scheeben (1835–1888).

For me, as a diocesan priest and someone who teaches and studies theology, there is just so much to love about Scheeben. I was introduced to Scheeben when I was doing my own doctoral work because the subject of my doctorate, Father John Courtney Murray, had written his own doctorate on Scheeben, titled "Matthias Joseph Scheeben's Doctrine on Supernatural Divine Faith."[2] Scheeben studied at the German national seminary in Rome and the Gregorian University as a young man and taught for a number of years in the diocesan seminary in Cologne. It's kind of hard to place Scheeben into one "school" of thought. As one of my own students said, he really is his own thing![3]

What I find most fascinating about Scheeben is that he was not only a premier theologian but also a mystic who stated that the purpose of his theology was "to make the Christian feel happy about his faith. Because the beauty and eminence of our faith consist in this: that through the mysteries of grace it raises our nature to an immeasurably high plane and presents to us an inexpressibly intimate union with God."[4] His text *The Mysteries of Christianity* presents a manual of understanding the Catholic faith that has influenced many thinkers of all types, from Réginald Garrigou-Lagrange to Hans Urs von Balthasar to Pope Benedict XVI. Scheeben writes: "A truth that is easily discovered and quickly grasped can neither enchant nor hold. To enchant and hold us it must surprise us by its novelty, it must overpower us with its magnificence; its wealth and profundity must exhibit ever new splendors, ever deeper abysses to the exploring eye."[5] Pope Pius XI, in an address to the seminarians of the German

College in Rome, described Scheeben as a "man of genius," stating: "He was a model of theology, and a model of spirited defense of the Church, the Holy See, and the Pope. Above all, he was a model of saintly Christian life."[6]

For Scheeben, everything in life is connected. His understanding of the great mysteries of the Faith is vast and deep. All the doctrines of the Church make sense because they are part of a whole system. He writes: "The light derived from the consideration of each separate mystery spreads automatically far and wide over the inner relationship and the wonderful harmony pervading them all, and thus the individual pictures take their places in an orderly gallery, which comprises everything magnificent and sublime that theology possesses far in excess of all the other sciences, including even philosophy."[7]

When reading *The Mysteries of Christianity*, I was brought back to an earlier moment in my own life and studies. I was a third-year seminarian at the Gregorian University and was sitting in a class on eschatology, listening to the professor rattle on in Italian, when all of a sudden I had a "Eureka!" moment. I understood that all of the moments in salvation history — from the creation of the world, to the Fall of man, to the struggles of the Chosen People, to the Immaculate Conception of the Blessed Virgin Mary, to the coming of the Messiah in the Incarnation, to the paschal mystery of Christ, to the coming *eschaton* — all of them are connected. And then, all at once, in a flash of insight, I realized that all of the moral teachings of the Church make logical sense if we take seriously the fact that everything is created, freely and gratuitously, by God out of love. Human beings were created in God's image and likeness and — despite the very real effects of the Fall (which was only possible because God made humans free, as he himself is free), with its consequences of original and actual sin — never lose their fundamental goodness and dignity. We cannot save ourselves from the consequences of the

Fall, and so we need a Redeemer, one who is like us in all things but sin, and that Redeemer is Christ. The Church is the spotless Bride of Christ, and she inheres in the world, especially in and through the sacraments, as his presence in the world. In order to be a member of his Mystical Body, we need to conform our lives and wills to his teachings, which come to us in the fonts of Divine Revelation (Sacred Scripture and Sacred Tradition) and are clarified in the Church's Magisterium.

> **All of the moral teachings of the Church make logical sense if we take seriously the fact that everything is created, freely and gratuitously, by God out of love.**

This simple act of recognizing the importance of theology and the unity of the Church's teachings to my prayer and life came rather late in my seminary formation, but I am grateful that it came. Theology became not simply a rote subject to pass in order to be ordained a priest but an invitation to explore a whole new world of meaning. (Please note that I do not claim to grasp the meanings of the mysteries of the Faith completely, or to be able to discern all of the wonderful interconnectedness they contain. I pray that, please God, if I make it to the beatific vision, I will understand more!)

I undergo this same experience when I read the works of Scheeben. He describes dogmatic theology as "speculative theology," seeing it as a theology that looks deeply into the truths of the Faith.[8] His theology is one of solid, clear rationality, combined with what Marshall describes as a "God-intoxication,"[9] and it is always in search of the harmony and interconnectedness of the Church's thought. Scheeben's work on Mariology (the historical, spiritual, and systematic study of the Blessed Mother), Christ's beatific vision, and the reality of God's grace — all done with academic precision in the midst of a prayerful life — prove a basic truth: Holiness of life must precede good, orthodox theology.

Some Practical Tips for Personal Study

1. Place a Cross on Your Desk

See your desk, your workspace, or wherever you study as your own private altar where you make a sacrifice. At the altar of your desk, you sacrifice yourself. As the Lord Jesus opens his arms wide on the cross in an embrace of love, so, too, must the student. As students, we sacrifice many things — most importantly our time and, what is most difficult, our own pride.

First, the sacrifice of time. Studying takes time! It means not doing other things that are really good and fun but aren't for you when you have to work. Sit yourself down, open the book and read, and don't forget to take some notes.

Second, pride. Studying can lead to changing our minds! In reading, we open ourselves up to having our worldviews changed. When I was teaching seminarians in a first-year theology class, I had a student who opined: "Father, I really don't like Aquinas. He's all reason and no spirituality. Thomas is all about philosophy and proofs and he never mentions Sacred Scripture and spirituality. Give me Augustine! He's all about passion and prayer and never gets abstract!" I was stunned. I asked him if he had actually read either of these theologians. He admitted that he had not read much of them at all. I asked the seminarian if he realized that Thomas Aquinas was primarily a scriptural commentator and that he was a deeply mystical thinker. And as for Augustine not being complex, I mentioned that he need not worry — we would read *De Trinitate* later that year. Now he was stunned! All he had thought was not quite accurate, and all of his presumptions were challenged. As it turned out, by the end of the class, this young seminarian had proved to be one of the finest, most reasonable students in my class, one who truly began to appreciate not only Saint Thomas and Saint Augustine, but all the Catholic Church's teachings. He had, like all of us do, a long way to go. I know that I must sacrifice myself daily on the altar of my desk because I want to know more and more about the One I love, the Lord Jesus, and about his Bride, the Church.

2. Pray to God the Holy Spirit for Enlightenment

When we study, we must turn to the Holy Spirit of God. It is the Lord, the giver of life, who imparts to us his sevenfold gifts — wisdom, understanding, counsel, fortitude, knowledge, piety, and fear of the Lord. Ask the Third Person of the Most Blessed Trinity to give you the gift of peace before, during, and after studying:

> Incomprehensible Creator, the true Fountain of light and only Author of all knowledge: vouchsafe, we beseech Thee, to enlighten our understandings, and to remove from us all darkness of sin and ignorance. Thou, who makest eloquent the tongues of those that want utterance, direct our tongues, and pour on our lips the grace of Thy blessing. Give us a diligent and obedient spirit, quickness of apprehension, capacity of retaining, and the powerful assistance of Thy holy grace; that what we hear or learn we may apply to Thy honor and the eternal salvation of our own souls.

*Ask the Holy Spirit to give you the gift of peace
before, during, and after studying.*

3. Turn to Saint Thomas Aquinas

The *Doctor Communis* is the patron saint of academics, schools, philosophers, and theologians. Turn to him for guidance! Saint Thomas is a heavenly patron for all of us who study, even if we are not "confirmed Thomists." Here is his prayer before study:

> Creator of all things, true source of light and wisdom, origin of all being, graciously let a ray of your light penetrate the darkness of my understanding. Take from me the double darkness in which I have been born, an obscurity of sin and ignorance. Give me a keen understanding, a retentive memory, and the ability to grasp things correctly and fundamentally. Grant me the talent of being exact in my explanations and the ability to express myself with thoroughness and charm. Point out the beginning, direct the progress, and help in the completion. I ask this through Jesus Christ our Lord. Amen.

Conclusion

We have covered a great deal of ground in this chapter and delved into what holiness is for the theologian. Through examples from Sacred Scripture and from the lives of two particular theologians, Thomas Aquinas and Matthias Joseph Scheeben — one a saint and the other whose cause for canonization has been introduced — we have seen that holiness of life leads one to want to attain the true wisdom that only the Lord can give. We have demonstrated as well that theology, done in faithfulness to the teachings of the Church, can lead to holiness of life. Perhaps it is most fitting to end this chapter with a prayer as we reflect on the gift of our faith from the Lord — a prayer that has been offered by many Catholics over many years:

> *Act of Faith*
> O my God, I firmly believe
> that you are one God in three divine Persons,
> Father, Son, and Holy Spirit.
> I believe that your divine Son became man

and died for our sins and that he will come
to judge the living and the dead.
I believe these and all the truths
which the Holy Catholic Church teaches
because you have revealed them
who are eternal truth and wisdom,
who can neither deceive nor be deceived.
In this faith I intend to live and die.
Amen.

Act of Hope
O Lord God,
I hope by your grace for the pardon
of all my sins
and after life here to gain eternal happiness
because you have promised it
who are infinitely powerful, faithful, kind,
and merciful.
In this hope I intend to live and die.
Amen.

Act of Love
O Lord God, I love you above all things
and I love my neighbor for your sake
because you are the highest, infinite and perfect
good, worthy of all my love.
In this love I intend to live and die.
Amen.

Praying is what makes the study of theology a personal encounter
with the Word of God rather than merely an academic pursuit.
As theologians, we sacrifice ourselves daily on the altars of our
desks, on the altars of our apostolic works, and on the altars of

our prayers. That's what it means to be a theologian in the class-room, in the streets, and in the chapel. That's the joy of studying theology!

Points to Remember

- True wisdom is the goal of all study.
- Good theology leads to holiness of life.

Suggestions for Further Reading

For further reading concerning topics in this chapter, you might want to consult the following:

- *Catechism of the Catholic Church*
- Bishop Robert Barron, *Thomas Aquinas: Spiritual Master* (New York: Crossroads, 1996), 13–29.
- Saint Thomas Aquinas, *Summa Theologiae* (I, q.1, a.6).
- Matthias Joseph Scheeben, *The Mysteries of Christianity* (New York: Crossroad, 2008).

Postscript

At the end of the Second Extraordinary Synod on the Family in 2015, Pope Francis offered an exhortation that received a standing ovation from the bishops. His advice was offered most immediately to bishops but can be taken as sage advice for all students of Catholic theology:

> Since a Synod is a journey of human beings, with the consolations there were also moments of desolation, of tensions and temptations, of which a few possibilities could be mentioned:
>
> - One, a temptation to hostile inflexibility, that is, wanting to close oneself within the written word, (the letter) and not allowing oneself to be surprised by God, by the God of surprises, (the spirit); within the law, within the certitude of what we know and not of what we still need to learn and to achieve. From the time of Christ, it is the temptation of the zealous, of the scrupulous, of the solicitous and of the so-called — to-

day — "traditionalists" and also of the intellectuals.

- The temptation to a destructive tendency to a superficial goodness that in the name of a deceptive mercy binds the wounds without first curing them and treating them; that treats the symptoms and not the causes and the roots. It is the temptation of the "do-gooders," of the fearful, and also of the so-called "progressives and liberals."

- The temptation to transform stones into bread to break the long, heavy, and painful fast (cf. Lk 4:1–4); and also to transform the bread into a stone and cast it against the sinners, the weak, and the sick (cf. Jn 8:7), that is, to transform it into unbearable burdens (Lk 11:46).

- The temptation to come down off the Cross, to please the people, and not stay there, in order to fulfill the will of the Father; to bow down to a worldly spirit instead of purifying it and bending it to the Spirit of God.

- The temptation to neglect the *depositum fidei* [the Deposit of Faith], not thinking of themselves as guardians but as owners or masters [of it]; or, on the other hand, the temptation to neglect reality, making use of meticulous language and a language of smoothing to say so many things and to say nothing![1]

Acknowledgments

I am immensely grateful to Mary Beth Giltner of Our Sunday Visitor Press for reaching out to me to write this text, as I am also to Heidi Saxton of Ave Maria Press for first connecting me with Mary Beth, who has proven to be a great guide and support. Laurie Malashanko was a tremendous editor and a wonderful dialogue partner in the preparation of this text.

In addition, thanks must be given to Kevin C. Knight of the *National Catholic Register*, who graciously allows me to be one of his correspondents. Readers of the *National Catholic Register* online will note that many of the chapters in this book have their origins in pieces of mine published there. Likewise, I am grateful to Edward Wilkinson, editor emeritus, and Jorge I. Dominguez, editor of the Diocese of Brooklyn's weekly newspaper, *The Tablet*. I have been blessed to be a columnist for *The Tablet* for almost twenty years, and many of the ideas in this book originated in articles I published in that newspaper.

Having the opportunity to serve as academic dean of the Pontifical North American College, the seminary for U.S. students in Rome, is a joy. Teaching the first-year introduction to theology seminar to the young men at the Pontifical Gregorian University has been one of the highlights of my priesthood. I am very grateful to the Very Reverend Peter C. Harman, the rector of the Pontifical North American College, and my colleagues in priestly formation at the seminary, especially Father John Geary McDonald, Father Randy Soto De Jesus, and Father Walter Riordan Oxley, who have been excellent dialogue partners for me in this project. Of course, I would also like to thank the seminarians whom I have been blessed to teach in my first-year class, with a particular thanks to those young men who have served as my "beadles" (class assistants) over the years: Joseph Mominee, Stephen Yusko, Oscar Romero Marquina, and Jose Lim. In addition, I thank Father Joseph Carola, SJ, and Father Nicolas Steeves, SJ, of the Pontifical Gregorian University, for permitting me to teach classes to both North American College students and international students at the Gregorian University itself.

In addition, Sister Mary Christa Nutt, RSM, Sister Mary Patrice Ahearn, RSM, and Sister Mary Angelica Neenan, OP, dear friends all, have been so very helpful to me while I was writing this text and in keeping me close to the Lord by their examples. Thanks also must be given to all of the Religious Sisters of Mercy of Alma, Michigan, for their kind friendship, love, and prayers. These sisters are gifts of God to the Church.

My entire Catholic education I owe to my mother, Catherine Mary Flynn Cush. She can never fully appreciate my gratitude for this gift. She and my late father, Edward Joseph Cush, sent me to Holy Name of Jesus grade school in Brooklyn (now Saint Joseph the Worker Catholic Academy) and then to Cathedral Preparatory Seminary in Elmhurst, New York (now Cathedral Preparatory School and Seminary), where I was given a series of fine educations. It was at Cathedral Prep many years ago that I met some wonderful diocesan priests who taught full-time and inspired me to be the best man I could be, humanly, spiritually, intellectually, and pastorally. They have my immense gratitude. This continued in Cathedral College Seminary in Douglaston, New York, and later at the Pontifical North American College, where the example of my rector, His Eminence Timothy Michael Cardinal Dolan, Ph.D., was essential to my priestly formation. Finally, I wish to thank the Most Reverend Nicholas DiMarzio, Ph.D., D.D., for his fatherly encouragement in my academic pursuits. It was Bishop DiMarzio who, soon after he arrived in the diocese, assigned me to teach high school full-time, instilling in me my love of teaching. It was Bishop DiMarzio who assigned me to study for the doctorate in sacred theology in Rome and encouraged me to complete the degree when all I wanted to do was to give up on it. It was Bishop DiMarzio who permitted me to accept Bishop James F. Checchio's kind invitation to serve on the formation faculty of the Pontifical North American College. Bishop DiMarzio has always been an example of a learned, academic man who is practical and pastoral. He loves his priests, and he loves his people. I can attest to this personally. I thank him for his kindness to me on the occasion of his retirement.

Appendix One
Some Suggestions for Building a Catholic Library

I have to admit that I am not easily scandalized. Not to sound jaded or world-weary, but it takes an awful lot to shock me; yet as a very young priest, I was shaken to the core by a simple statement spoken by an older priest that unfortunately was not made in jest. He stated simply and clearly that, after his first three years of priesthood, he never wrote another homily. After all, he had in those first three years gone through the entire Lectionary cycle, and — although the translations of the readings have changed over the years — the content of the readings had not. Father had done his work in the 1970s and, more than twenty years later, reading off yellowing sheets of handwritten notes, was still living off the fruits of his labor. I was dumbfounded. I asked if he ever adapted them for the congregation to which he was preaching, and he replied in the negative. I asked if he ever incorporated anything new that the Church had articulated since the first few years of his priesthood, such as encyclicals or the *Catechism of the Catholic Church*. He again replied in the negative. He had done his work early on and that was that. I asked if he still read theology, and he said not since he left the seminary.

I know this sounds judgmental — and I don't want to be like the Pharisee who states: "'O God, I thank you that I am not like the rest of humanity ... " (Lk 18:11, NABRE) — but I have made a pledge never to be like that, to always try to update my homilies, even if some (or even most) of my thoughts on the Sacred Scriptures remain the same over time. Looking around the priest's room where we sat, I noticed that he didn't have a single book in his room, not a one. I then recalled the words of a spiritual director at the college seminary I attended: "Beware the priest who has *no books* in his room, because he's probably not keeping up with his intellectual formation. Also beware the priest who has *lots of books* in his room without the binding being cracked on any of them, because he has allowed himself to become just a book collector." (Yes, I realize we can have many books digitally today, but this was said years ago!) I made a pledge to keep up with my intellectual formation as a young priest and not to be just a dilettante who collects books and never reads them. And I have found that having a good, basic theological library has been a blessing in my life as a Catholic Christian, as a believer, and as a priest.

May I offer suggestions of some books that you might want to have in your personal Catholic library? Keep in mind that these are suggestions for the very basic, necessary books.

1. A good Catholic study Bible in English — For me, the *Ignatius Bible: Revised Standard Version — Second Catholic Edition* (Ignatius Press, 2005) is a jewel to be treasured. The *Ignatius Catholic Study Bible: New Testament* (Ignatius Press, 2010) has some excellent notes by Dr. Scott Hahn and Curtis Mitch, and Ignatius Press also publishes a large number of study Bibles for the Old Testament with some solid, orthodox notes.

2. The *Catechism of the Catholic Church* — This is absolutely essential for a theological library. Be sure to get the second edition of the *Catechism* from 1997! The *Companion to the Catechism of the Catholic Church* and the *Compendium of the Catechism of the Catholic Church* are also very helpful for someone creating a theological library.

3. *Enchiridion Symbolorum: A Compendium of Creeds, Definitions, and Declarations of the Catholic Church* (Ignatius Press, 2012; combined Latin and English edition) — This is a great collection of the main texts of the Catholic Church. The new 2012 edition takes the reader through the pontificate of Pope Benedict XVI and includes many (though not all) of the magisterial documents. None of Pope Francis's work has appeared yet in an English edition, but hopefully it will soon. His teaching does appear on the Vatican's website at http://w2.vatican.va/content/vatican/en.html.

4. *The Documents of Vatican II, with Notes and Index: Vatican Translation* (Alba House, 2009) —This edition offers the sixteen documents of the Council along with study notes and a handy index. A Catholic should know what Vatican II actually states, not just what other people say it states!

5. *Summa Theologica* by Saint Thomas Aquinas — A brand-new edition brings this massive but essential work into one volume (824 pages, with small print) in Jake E. Stief's *Summa Theologica: The Only Complete and Unabridged Edition in One Volume* (2017). There are, of course, many different editions one could choose for the *Summa*, but this is a new and concise one. A good introductory guide might be Peter Kreeft's *A Shorter Summa: The Essential Philosophical Passages of Saint Thomas Aquinas' Summa Theologica* (Ignatius Press, 1993). Saint Thomas's thought is a building block for Catholic theology.

6. *Introduction to Christianity: Revised Edition* by Cardinal Joseph Ratzinger (Ignatius Press, 2004; first published in 1968) — This classic sets the scene for an understanding of late twentieth-century Catholic theology. The product of the future pope's study and work as a young professor following his involvement in Vatican II, this book sets the reader on a proper path for the study of theology.

7. *The Shape of Catholic Theology: An Introduction to Its Sources, Principles, and History* by Aidan Nichols (Liturgical Press, 1991) — This is, in my opinion, the best introduction to the study of theology for any student. It is a book that I have used since I was beginning my own theological studies, and it is one that I use today as a professor. It offers a proper understanding of the fonts of Divine Revelation, namely Sacred Scripture and Sacred Tradition, as well as an understanding of the Church's Magisterium. It is a clear, very readable introduction.

8. *Beginning to Read the Fathers: Revised Edition* by Boniface Ramsey (Paulist Press, 2012) — This volume gives a thematic overview of the great thinkers of the patristic period. It might inspire the reader to study the Fathers of the Church themselves.

9. *The Encyclicals of John Paul II: An Introduction and Commentary* by Richard A. Spinello (Rowman & Littlefield, 2016) — This is a masterful edition of the thought of this great saint, who I pray will one day be a Doctor of the Church.

10. *Christian Spirituality in the Catholic Tradition* by Jordan Aumann (Ignatius Press, 1985) — Check out this great introduction to some wonderful spiritual writers and their theology. It will whet the reader's appetite to know more about our great saints, from the early Church to the post-Tridentine period to the twentieth century.

11. *The Mysteries of Christianity* by Matthias J. Scheeben (Crossroad, 2008) — Father Scheeben was a nineteenth-century German Roman Catholic who was a premier theologian and a mystic. He stated that the purpose of his theology was "to make the Christian feel happy about his faith. Because the beauty and eminence of our faith consist in this: that through the mysteries of grace it raises our nature to an immeasurably high plane and presents to us an inexpressibly intimate union with God." This work presents a manual for understanding the Catholic Faith and has influenced successive thinkers of all types, from Réginald Garrigou-Lagrange to Hans Urs von Balthasar. Scheeben writes; "A truth that is easily discovered and quickly grasped can neither enchant nor hold. To enchant and hold us it must surprise us by its novelty, it must overpower us with its magnificence; its wealth and profundity must exhibit ever new splendors, ever deeper abysses to the exploring eye." That is precisely what his text helps us to do.

12. *The Lord* by Romano Guardini (Gateway, 2012) — This text seamlessly melds deep spirituality with fine dogmatic theology, and it was a prime impetus for Pope Benedict XVI's *Jesus of Nazareth* series. Father Guardini, now a Servant of God, offers his readers an unforgettable experience of the Lord that touches the mind and the heart.

13. *Theology of Revelation* by René Latourelle (Wipf & Stock, 2009) — Father René Latourelle, SJ, who recently passed away, was a French-Canadian Jesuit who taught for years at the Gregorian University in Rome. He is, in my opinion, the author of the premier book on understanding the theology of Revelation according to the fonts of Divine Revelation, as interpreted through the Magisterium of the Church. Latourelle is the father of our contemporary understanding of the discipline of fundamental theology (which includes the study of the fonts of Divine Revelation, the transmission of Divine Revelation, and the credibility of Divine Revelation). This text is a treasure.

14. *Meeting Christ in the Sacraments* by Colman O'Neill (Alba House, 2014; first published 1964) — Father O'Neill's text is one that is very underappreciated today. It is a book about how we receive God's grace in and through the sacraments of the Holy Church. A Dominican friar who taught at the University of Fribourg, he gave one of the clearest syntheses of the sacraments in an age (the 1960s) where confusion was abounding in several circles, especially regarding the sacraments. For many years, Father O'Neill's "sacramental realism" has helped to clarify questions I have had myself, as well as ones I have received in the course of my ministry as a priest and teacher.

15. *Rekindling the Christic Imagination* by Robert Imbelli (Liturgical Press, 2014) — I consider Father Robert Imbelli to be one of the finest minds in the American Roman Catholic Church, and I am proud to say that he is a diocesan priest from New York! A true professor in the best sense of the word (one who professes the truth), Father Imbelli has written a gem of a book that is as contemporary as it is timeless. Illustrated with fine art and using examples from some of the best of Western culture, this book engages the mind, heart, and soul of his readers in a true theological formation.

16. *And Now I See … A Theology of Transformation* by Robert Barron (Crossroad, 1998) — One of Bishop Barron's very first books, this volume remains my favorite. Reading this text as a seminarian made me want to be a priest who is in love with Christ, in love with theology, and fully engaged in the culture for the sake of evangelization. In this dialogue with literature, film, art, music, philosophy, theology, and psychology, Bishop Barron taught me that "above all else, Christianity is a matter of seeing." The bishop, through his writing, taught me to see Christ in my theological studies and always to use theology for the pastoral growth of the People of God.

17. *Jesus Christ: Fundamentals of Christology* by Roch Kereszty (Alba House, 2002) — This is my "go-to" book when it comes to the most important Person in my life, my Savior, Jesus Christ. Father Kereszty, a Cistercian professor at the University of Dallas, gives what I believe is the best synthesis of the study of who Jesus is (what we call the theological discipline of Christology) with the study of what Jesus does (that he is Savior — the theological discipline of soteriology) available in English. This book will be a treasure in your library.

18. *The Trinity: An Introduction to the Catholic Doctrine on the Triune God* by Gilles Emery (Catholic University of America, 2012) — Father Emery's book takes the really complicated subject of God himself and defines the terms that Catholic theology uses in a useful and handy glossary. As far as I am concerned, this is the best basic text on the Most Blessed Trinity.

19. *Saint Thomas Aquinas, Volumes One (The Person and His Work)* and *Two (Spiritual Master)* by Jean-Pierre Torrell (Catholic University of America, 2005 [vol. 1] and 2003 [vol. 2]) — I have to admit that a major *lacuna* in my studies is the theology of Saint Thomas Aquinas. Bad philosophy leads to bad theology, and when I was studying philosophy in the early 1990s in college seminary, not much time at all was given to Saint Thomas. We read a great deal about how others, especially Bernard Lonergan, SJ, and Frederick Copleston, SJ, understood him, but I can say that I never really engaged Saint Thomas himself until I began doctoral studies. Dominican Father Torrell's two-volume work gives a tremendous introduction to the life of Saint Thomas and his theology. I can tell you that I need to read more *of* Saint Thomas, rather than just *about* him, but these volumes really helped me "know that I did not know."

20. *Introduction to Theological Method* by Jared Wicks (Piemme, 1994) — The method laid out in this edition, since updated as *Doing Theology* (Paulist, 2009), was the way that I learned to study theology. Father Wicks, my professor for my introductory class in fundamental theology many years ago at the Gregorian University in Rome, is currently a scholar in residence at the Pontifical College Josephinum in Ohio. This text gives an easily grasped overview of the concept of Divine Revelation and its two fonts — Sacred Scripture and Sacred Tradition — as well as the roles that the Magisterium and positive theology play in the Church's theology. Wicks's genetic method is "fair and balanced," to use a quote from television, and I think it is a remarkably fine text. In many ways, it complements well Aidan Nichols's work *The Shape of Catholic Theology*, mentioned above. Both books were written around the same time by professors in Rome at two Roman pontifical universities (Wicks taught at the Gregorian and Nichols at the Angelicum), and both are excellent introductory textbooks. I am very grateful to have studied theology in the time and place at which I did, and these are both seminal texts for me.

Appendix Two
Building a Library of Catholic Spiritual Classics

My criteria for these suggestions were simple. First, what books have helped me grow spiritually? Second, what books do I think might be generally helpful to Catholic people today?

1. *Confessions* by Saint Augustine — There are many editions and translations out there, but I would recommend a recent translation by Sister Maria Boulding, OSB, edited by Father David Meconi, SJ (Ignatius Press, 2012). In the English language, the word "doctor" has two meanings: one, a learned person who, through study, has learned and can teach what he's learned; and two, a healer. Doctor, teacher, and healer are three roles that the great Augustine of Hippo, bishop and Doctor of the Church, exemplifies. In many ways, Augustine is the model of what it means to be human, and his *Confessions* details his journey to becoming a human truly alive in Christ. Painfully aware of the effects of original sin in the world, Augustine understands what Saint Paul the apostle states

in his Letter to the Romans: "What I do, I do not understand. For I do not do what I want, but I do what I hate" (7:15, NABRE). In the second book of his *Confessions*, Augustine recognizes that sin at its essence is nothing more than what patristic scholar Father David Meconi, SJ, describes as "self-sabotage." Augustine tells the story of when he was a young man and he and his friends, in an act of adolescent mischief, stole some pears. He stole them even though he really didn't want them. Augustine writes: "My desire was to enjoy not what I sought by stealing but merely the excitement of thieving and the doing of what was wrong. There was a pear tree near our vineyard laden with fruit, though attractive in neither color nor taste. To shake the fruit off the tree and carry off the pears, I and a gang of naughty adolescents set off late at night. … We carried off a huge load of pears. But they were not for our feasts but merely to throw to the pigs" (2.4.9).

Augustine, the Doctor, understands sin as much as one can understand the absurd, which is what sin ultimately is. God has given us the path, whereas we choose to go our own way. He gives us the means to fly, and we choose to crawl. This Doctor of the Church knows our fallen human nature. He writes: "I became evil for no reason. I had no motive for my wickedness except wickedness itself. It was foul, and I loved it. I loved the self-destruction, I loved my fall, not the object for which I had fallen but my fall itself. My depraved soul leaped down from your firmament to ruin. I was seeking not to gain anything by shameful means, but shame for its own sake." How often are we like this in our lives? You see, there's a right thing to do and a wrong thing to do in life, and in most cases, it's fairly obvious. To say that there are shades of gray in a situation is to admit that there exist black and white, good and evil. In and through prayer, through developing a Catholic conscience, we learn what is sin and what is virtue. But like the young Augustine, we fall into sin, suffering the threefold alienation that sin is — alienation from God, from others, and from ourselves. And only in a threefold reconciliation with God, others, and self, a reconciliation that comes in the shape of the cross of grace, do we find peace.

And yet it is his knowledge, his experience of life, that leads the Doctor to be a healer. Augustine knows that the human heart is restless until it rests in God. He knows that all is grace and that we are totally, completely dependent on God. He trusts that even a poor sinner like himself, a sinner like you and me, never loses the image of being created in the likeness of God — even though original sin distorts the image. Christ comes to save. Augustine learned again and again that the divided self can be healed only through, with, and in Christ Jesus. And in his ministry as bishop and as pastor, he offered that healing — the healing that only the presence of grace, the free and undeserved gift of God in our lives, can bring. We are sinners, redeemed by God's grace, and need to make our prayer that of Augustine: "You called and cried out loud and shattered my deafness. You were radiant and resplendent, you put to flight my blindness. You were fragrant, and I drew in my breath and now pant after you. I tasted you, and I feel but hunger and thirst for you. You touched me, and I am set on fire to attain the peace which is yours." The *Confessions* is a book that can change your life!

2. *The Story of a Soul* by Saint Thérèse of Lisieux — As with the *Confessions*, you can find many different English translations and editions of this book. The one I recommend is *Story of a Soul: Study Edition*, translated by John Clarke, OCD, and prepared by Mark Foley, OCD (ICS Publications, 2005). Earlier in this book, I professed my great love for the Little Flower and her "little way," and mentioned why I believe her to be one of the greatest Doctors of the Church. I don't want to repeat that here. Suffice it to say, my recent pilgrimage to Lisieux with visits to the home where she was raised, the beautiful basilica erected in her honor (which contains her saintly parents' relics), and the Carmel where she herself is entombed, was a tremendous experience. To see and pray in the places that the Little Flower describes in her autobiography was truly moving. Her wisdom is beyond compare. Read her words, the words of a young nun who died at the age of twenty-four in 1897:

> I understand and I know from experience that: "The kingdom of God is within you." Jesus has no need of books or teachers to instruct souls; He teaches without the noise of words. Never have I heard Him speak, but I feel that He is within me at each moment; He is guiding and inspiring me with what I must say and do. I find just when I need them certain lights that I had not seen until then, and it isn't most frequently during my hours of prayer that these are most abundant but rather in the midst of my daily occupations. (179)

Simple, lovely, practical, and holy — the Little Flower is as much a Doctor of the Church as Augustine. Both are healers and wise persons.

3. *The Seven Storey Mountain* by Thomas Merton — I would recommend the fiftieth anniversary edition from Harcourt, published in 1999, with an introduction by Robert Giroux. This will, no doubt, be a controversial choice in this list of spiritual classics. I contend that the early Merton, in books such as *The Seven Storey Mountain* (1948) and *The Sign of Jonas* (1953), offers insights into the spiritual life of a man of the world who became a Trappist and into a unique time in the history of the Roman Catholic Church in the United States. I have some serious reservations, however, about some of Merton's later writings. To be honest, I put off reading this book for many years. When I was in the seminary, Thomas Merton was not read at all; he was, in fact, more famous for his unfortunate death than for any profound spiritual insights. A fine priest who was my spiritual director at the time suggested I read *The Seven Storey Mountain* while on retreat at the Trappist Saint Joseph's Abbey in Spencer, Massachusetts. I took his advice, and I am very glad that I did.

Merton's journey may not resonate with everyone, and some may find his writing style a bit indulgent, but I can assure you that his insights into the Catholic faith, detailed at this early stage of his vocation, are priceless. Read what Merton, then known as Father Louis (his religious name) has to say about the Eucharist in *The Seven Storey Mountain*:

> I did not even know who Christ was, that He was God. I had not the faintest idea that there existed such a thing as the Blessed Sacrament. I thought churches were simply places where people got together and sang a few hymns. And yet now I tell you, you who are now what I once was, unbelievers, it is that Sacrament, and that alone, the Christ living in our midst, and sacrificed by us, and for us and with us, in the clean and perpetual Sacrifice, it is He alone Who holds our world together, and keeps us all from being poured headlong and immediately into the pit of our eternal destruction. And I tell you there is a power that goes forth from that Sacrament, a power of light and truth, even into the hearts of those who have heard nothing of Him and seem to be incapable of belief. (41)

Merton's autobiography of faith is well worth reading. Here, he describes a conversation that he has with his friend Lax shortly after his conversion to Catholicism:

"What do you want to want to be, anyway?"

"I don't know; I guess what I want to be is a good Catholic."

"What you should say" — he told me — "what you should say is that you want to be a saint." (238)

Don't we all?

4. *He Leadeth Me: An Extraordinary Testament of Faith* by Servant of God Walter J. Ciszek, SJ, with Daniel L. Flaherty, SJ (Ignatius, 2014; first published in 1973) — This extraordinary book is the story of an American priest who was captured by the Russians in World War II, charged with being a spy for the Vatican, and sent to Siberia to work in a labor camp. He was there for fifteen years. In the midst of brutality, he was able to offer his pain and suffering to Christ, and he grew in prayer, in faith, and in his priesthood. There is so much in *He Leadeth Me* from which a Catholic can learn. Father Ciszek writes: "No matter how close to God the soul felt, how blessed it was by an awareness of his presence on occasion, the realities of life were always at hand, always demanding recognition, always demanding acceptance. I had continuously to learn to accept God's will — not as I wished it to be, not as it might have been, but as it actually was at the moment. And it was through the struggle to do this that spiritual growth and a greater appreciation of his will took place" (188).

This is a great book about trusting in God's providence, something that I, as a chronic worrier and compulsive planner, have a very hard time doing. This great Servant of God also writes:

Across that threshold I had been afraid to cross, things suddenly seemed so very simple. There was but a single vision, God, who was all in all; there was but one will that directed all things, God's will. I had only to see it, to discern it in every circumstance in which I found myself and let myself be ruled by it. God is in all things, sustains all things, directs all things. To discern this in every situation and circumstance, to see His will in all things, was to accept each circumstance and situation and let oneself be borne along in perfect confidence and trust. Nothing could separate me from Him, because He was in all things. (79)

Certainly good advice for worried Christians!

5. *The Book of Pastoral Rule* by Saint Gregory the Great — This is a real gem, and I urge not only priests and religious but all Christian people to read this sixth-century patristic text. The edition I recommend is from the Popular Patristics Series, translated by George Demacopoulos, and published by St. Vladimir's Seminary Press in 2007. Pope Saint Gregory was, above all, a priest and a bishop, and the advice that he gives is applicable to pastoral ministry today. This Doctor of the Church was on fire with the love of God for souls. In a troubled age such as ours, Pope Saint Gregory the Great is a guide to the ordained and a comfort to the lay and religious faithful. He writes: "No one does more harm in the Church than he who has the title or rank of holiness and acts perversely" (32); and he further states that "those who do not speak the words of God with humility must be advised that when they apply medicine to the sick, they must first inspect the poison of their own infection, or else by attempting to heal others, they kill themselves" (159).

6. *Introduction to the Devout Life* by Saint Francis de Sales — This true classic, first published in 1609, offers sublime wisdom about living as a Christian in the world. There are, of course, many different editions available in English. I recommend Vintage Press's 2002 edition with an introduction by the late Cardinal Edward

Egan of New York. Saint Francis is a powerful, pastoral, practical saint. Writing as bishop of a large, diverse diocese in an area overrun by the effects of the Protestant Reformation, he offers great advice and can serve as a real spiritual director, even for those of us in the twenty-first century. Delving right into the truth of our human condition in our fallen world, he writes: "Ordinary purification, whether of body or soul, is only accomplished by slow degrees, step by step, gradually and painfully" and also "Do not … let us be disheartened by our imperfections. Our very perfection lies in diligently contending against them, and it is impossible so to contend without seeing them, or to overcome without meeting them face-to-face" (12). The key for Saint Francis de Sales is humility rooted in the truth.

7. *The Rule of Saint Benedict* — The longer I am a diocesan priest, the more I come to the opinion that the religious priests most similar to us are the Benedictines. Throughout my priesthood, I have been blessed to know, minister with, and learn from some fine Benedictine monks, and I have learned some valuable lessons on living the Christian life from those who live the Rule of Saint Benedict. There are, as with all of the books on this list, many editions of the Rule available. One version I have found very helpful is Benedictine Abbot Patrick Barry's 2004 edition from HiddenSpring Press. There is so much in the Rule that religious, clergy, and the lay faithful can learn from. One thing that particularly resonates with me is what Benedict writes about obedience in chapter five:

> This very obedience, however, will be acceptable to God and agreeable to men only if compliance with what is commanded is not cringing or sluggish or half-hearted, but free from any grumbling or any reaction of unwillingness. For the obedience shown to superiors is given to

God, as he himself said: Whoever listens to you, listens to me (Luke 10:16). Furthermore, the disciples' obedience must be given gladly, for God loves a cheerful giver (2 Cor 9:7). If a disciple obeys grudgingly and grumbles, not only aloud but also in his heart, then, even though he carries out the order, his action will not be accepted with favor by God, who sees that he is grumbling in his heart. He will have no reward for service of this kind; on the contrary, he will incur punishment for grumbling, unless he changes for the better and makes amends.

8. *The Dialogue* by Saint Catherine of Siena — One of the finest of the Doctors of the Church, Catherine is a model for all those who want to see true reform in the Church and who want to live their own unique vocations well. Saint Catherine, a lay Dominican who lived in the fourteenth century, sought *Veritas* (Truth); and she knew that it was only to be found with, through, and in her love, Jesus, who is Truth itself. She writes down a powerful conversation she had with the Lord:

> Know, dearest daughter, how, by humble, continual, and faithful prayer, the soul acquires, with time and persever-ance, every virtue. Wherefore should she persevere and never abandon prayer, either through the illusion of the Devil or her own fragility, that is to say, either on account of any thought or movement coming from her own body, or of the words of any creature. The Devil often places himself upon the tongues of creatures, causing them to chatter nonsensically, with the purpose of preventing the prayer of the soul. All of this she should pass by, by means of the virtue of perseverance. Oh, how sweet and pleasant to that soul and to Me is holy prayer, made in the house of knowledge of self and of Me, opening the

eye of the intellect to the light of faith, and the affections to the abundance of My charity, which was made visible to you, through My visible only-begotten Son, who showed it to you with His Blood! Which Blood inebriates the soul and clothes her with the fire of divine charity, giving her the food of the Sacrament [which is placed in the tavern of the mystical body of the Holy Church] that is to say, the food of the Body and Blood of My Son, wholly God and wholly man, administered to you by the hand of My vicar, who holds the key of the Blood. This is that tavern, which I mentioned to you, standing on the Bridge, to provide food and comfort for the travelers and the pilgrims, who pass by the way of the doctrine of My Truth, lest they should faint through weakness. This food strengthens little or much, according to the desire of the recipient, whether he receives sacramentally or virtually. He receives sacramentally when he actually communicates with the Blessed Sacrament. He receives virtually when he communicates, both by desire of communion, and by contemplation of the Blood of Christ crucified, communicating, as it were, sacramentally, with the affection of love, which is to be tasted in the Blood which, as the soul sees, was shed through love. On seeing this the soul becomes inebriated, and blazes with holy desire and satisfies herself, becoming full of love for Me and for her neighbor. Where can this be acquired? In the house of self-knowledge with holy prayer, where imperfections are lost, even as Peter and the disciples, while they remained in watching and prayer, lost their imperfection and acquired perfection. By what means is this acquired? By perseverance seasoned with the most holy faith. (Cosimo Classics Edition, Algar Thorold, translator; 159–160)

There is so much that one can glean from Saint Catherine.

9. *A Pilgrim's Journey: The Autobiography of Ignatius of Loyola* (Ignatius, 2004, with introduction, translation, and commentary by Joseph N. Tylenda, SJ) — This book offers a wonderful look into the mind and heart of the man who founded one of the most influential religious communities in the history of the Church — the Jesuits — and who gave us men who have shaped the intellectual, pastoral, and spiritual history of the world over the past 500 years. Ignatius, a sixteenth-century Spaniard and man of the world, felt called by the Lord to set the world on fire — with his passion, intellect, imagination, and will. In his heart, he was dedicated to being a soldier for Christ and a pilgrim. Saint Ignatius and his Spiritual Exercises have added a rich dimension to Catholic spirituality. I am very partial to Ignatius, having studied for many years at the Roman university that he founded, the Pontifical Gregorian University. Anyone who wishes to know the Catholic spiritual tradition cannot discount the role, example, and spiritual writings of the founder of the Society of Jesus.

10. *Albert and Thomas: Selected Writings* (translated, edited, and with an introduction by Simon Tugwell, OP, Paulist Press, 1988) — I would be remiss in listing anything in the Catholic life without including Saint Thomas Aquinas. This text is one that I have found helpful in understanding the *Doctor Communis* on prayer. It gathers together Saint Thomas's writings on prayer, along with those of his mentor, Saint Albert the Great, into a single, accessible volume. It includes selections from Saint Thomas's scriptural commentaries on Saint John, Saint Matthew, and Saint Paul, as well as items from the *Summa contra Gentiles*, the *Summa Theologiae*, *De Veritate*, and the *Sentences*.

Appendix Three
Building a Library of Catholic Fiction

One of the formative intellectual and spiritual periods of my life was when I was a college seminarian in the 1990s studying at St. John's University in New York. I was enrolled in a unique class titled "Catholic Novel" and taught by Father Robert Lauder. It was a truly interdisciplinary course that involved deeply Catholic theological and spiritual themes, was taught in the philosophy department, and required us to read works of literature. Taught by a dynamic and inspiring priest-professor and with a roster of around ten students, including laypeople, religious, and seminarians, it introduced me to some great stories that helped me to understand the mystery of God and his Church, and it really affected my human, spiritual, intellectual, and pastoral formation. Father Lauder now offers his class via a television series titled *The Catholic Novel* on NET TV (https://netny.tv/shows/the -catholic-novel/).

According to the series' website, Father Lauder describes a Catholic novel as "a story whose theme is directly related to a

Catholic dogmatic or moral teaching, or a Catholic sacramental principle, and in which the mystery of Catholicism is treated favorably." He goes on to state that unfortunately, in recent years the "Catholic novel has been like a treasure hidden in a field, largely neglected even by Catholics." I agree with his assessment.

In the spirit of the earlier appendixes on basic theological books and spiritual readings, I'll mention the Catholic novels that have most profoundly affected me.

1. *The Violent Bear It Away* (1960) by Flannery O'Connor — Flannery O'Connor is known chiefly as a short story writer. She uses a uniquely American, and a uniquely grotesque, style. She describes her work as follows:

> The novelist with Christian concerns will find in modern life distortions which are repugnant to him, and his problem will be to make these appear as distortions to an audience which is used to seeing them as natural; and he may well be forced to take ever more violent means to get his vision across to this hostile audience. When you can assume that your audience holds the same beliefs you do, you can relax a little and use more normal ways of talking to it; when you have to assume that it does not, then you have to make your vision apparent by shock — to the hard of hearing you shout, and for the almost blind you draw large and startling figures. (*Mystery and Manners*, 33–34)

The Violent Bear It Away is one of only two novels O'Connor wrote. It is the story of a young man, Francis Tarwater, who is raised by his uncle to be a "prophet." Flannery O'Connor, a good Catholic and a Thomist in her theology, offers a Catholic view of grace, of the sacraments, and of the need for faith and reason to be in harmony through her very Southern Evangelical Protestant characters. She writes:

> He felt his hunger no longer as a pain but as a tide. He felt it rising in himself through time and darkness, rising through the centuries, and he knew that it rose in a line of men whose lives were chosen to sustain it, who would wander in the world, strangers from that violent country where the silence is never broken except to shout the truth. He felt it building from the blood of Abel to his own, rising and engulfing him. It seemed in one instant to lift and turn him. He whirled toward the treeline. There, rising and spreading in the night, a red-gold tree of fire ascended as if it would consume the darkness in one tremendous burst of flame. The boy's breath went out to meet it. He knew that this was the fire that had encircled Daniel, that had raised Elijah from the earth, that had spoken to Moses and would in the instant speak to him. He threw himself to the ground and with his face against the dirt of the grave, he heard the command. GO WARN THE CHILDREN OF GOD OF THE TERRIBLE SPEED OF MERCY. The words were as silent as seeds opening one at a time in his blood. (242)

Flannery O'Connor might shock you, but she will never bore you!

2. *The Moviegoer* by Walker Percy (1961) is probably my favorite novel of all time, and Percy is my favorite novelist. He was a medical doctor, and his own story is fascinating, one of conversion to the Catholic faith through his reading of philosophy, especially Christian existentialism. *The Moviegoer*, another story set in the American South, takes place in New Orleans. It tells the tale of a young man, Binx Bolling, who lives a superficial life, defining himself through the films he watches and the deodorant he uses. Percy, an amazingly erudite writer, paints a picture with words, describing Binx's desire to love and be loved:

> He means that he hopes to find himself a girl, the rarest of rare pieces, and live the life of Rudolfo on the balcony, sitting around on the floor and experiencing soul-communications. I have my doubts. In the first place, he will defeat himself, jump ten miles ahead of himself, scare the wits out of some girl with his great choking silences, want her so desperately that by his own peculiar logic he can't have her; or having her, jump another ten miles beyond both of them and end by fleeing to the islands where, propped at the rail of his ship in some rancid port, he will ponder his own loneliness. (216)

Binx, through the love of a girl, Kate, discovers the love of God. This is a life-changing book.

3. Morris West, the Australian author of *The Shoes of the Fisherman* (1963), offers his best novel in *The Devil's Advocate* (1959). As one who lives and works in Rome, I truly love this novel. It tells the story of Monsignor Blaise Meredith, a British priest who works in the Vatican's Congregation for the Causes of Saints as the "Devil's Advocate," whose role it is to disprove the sanctity of those proposed for canonization. Monsignor Meredith, in his office job, has become a "professional" priest. West writes in his voice: "I feel the life slipping out of me. When the pain comes, I cry out, but there is no prayer in it, only fear. I kneel and recite my office and the Rosary but the words are empty — dry gourds rattling in the silence. The dark is terrible and I feel so alone. I see no signs but the symbols of contradiction. I try to dispose myself to faith, hope and charity, but my will is a blown reed in the winds of despair" (121). When he is sent to Calabria in Southern Italy to investigate the life of a young man, Giacomo Nerone, and meets the townsfolk, Meredith grows as a priest and as a man. This is a fine novel about the priesthood.

4. Another fine book about priesthood comes from Graham Greene in *The Power and the Glory* (1940). Set in the days of Mexico's suppression of the Catholic Church, *The Power and the Glory* tells the tale of the "Whiskey Priest," a fallen, craven man who, despite his own personal failings and real sins, is striving for repentance. Greene has him say: "But I'm a bad priest, you see. I know — from experience — how much beauty Satan carried down with him when he fell. Nobody ever said the fallen angels were the ugly ones" (168–169). The priest is a fugitive, a man on the run. And yet, though he tries to run from God and to shirk his duties, he is a priest, ontologically configured to Christ at the deepest part of his soul.

5. Georges Bernanos's *The Diary of a Country Priest* (1936) is a moving story of a young priest who is suffering, both with stomach cancer and with the lack of faith his parishioners continually exhibit, despite his best efforts. This is a beautiful story of grace, mercy, and redemption from which all people — Catholic and non-Catholic, religious, lay, and clergy — can benefit. Bernanos taught me a valuable lesson, that "the wish to pray is a prayer in itself." He writes further, on the nature of preaching:

> Teaching is no joke, sonny! ... Comforting truths, they call it! Truth is meant to save you first, and the comfort comes afterwards. Besides, you've no right to call that sort of thing comfort. Might as well talk about condolences! The Word of God is a red-hot iron. And you who preach it 'ud go picking it up with a pair of tongs, for fear

of burning yourself, you daren't get hold of it with both hands. It's too funny! Why, the priest who descends from the pulpit of Truth, with a mouth like a hen's vent, a little hot but pleased with himself, he's not been preaching: at best he's been purring like a tabby-cat. Mind you that can happen to us all, we're all half asleep, it's the devil to wake us up, sometimes — the apostles slept all right at Gethsemane. Still, there's a difference ... And mind you many a fellow who waves his arms and sweats like a furniture-remover isn't necessarily any more awakened than the rest. On the contrary. I simply mean that when the Lord has drawn from me some word for the good of souls, I know, because of the pain of it. (42)

6. Robert Hugh Benson's *The Lord of the World* (1907) is one of the finest novels I have ever read. I can still recall reading this novel over two days in the month prior to my priestly ordination, at the urging of my seminary spiritual director. Written by the convert son of the Anglican Archbishop of Canterbury, Edward White Benson, this is an early work written while he was the Catholic chaplain at Cambridge University. It is the story, broken into three parts, of the coming of the Antichrist in the world of the early twenty-first century. This is a world of secular humanism, a one-world religion, and a one-world government. Benson writes: "In the ages of faith a very inadequate grasp of religion would pass muster; in these searching days none but the humble and the pure could stand the test for long, unless indeed they were protected by a miracle of ignorance. The alliance of Psychology and Materialism did indeed seem, looked at from one angle, to account for everything; it needed a robust supernatural perception to understand their practical inadequacy." Both Pope Emeritus Benedict XVI and Pope Francis have urged Catholics to read this important, prophetic novel. The battle detailed in this novel, a battle between President Felsenburgh and Pope Sylvester III, between a materialistic world and a world that recognizes the presence of grace, is played out daily in our time. It's is a piece of fiction all Catholics should read.

7. Myles Connolly's *Mr. Blue* (1928) is the story of J. Blue, a modern-day Saint Francis figure, a man who is noble in his simplicity and able to see God's working in the world. It is a story of friendship, of God's love and mercy. This is a beautiful work, full of Connolly's eloquent prose:

> It is the humble man who risks his dignity to speak up for what he loves. It is the courageous man who dares contradiction and the acrimony of argument to defend his beliefs. If one loves anything, truth, beauty, woman, life, one will speak out. Genuine love cannot endure silence. Genuine love breaks out into speech. And when it is great love, it breaks out into song. Talk helps to relieve us of the tiresome burden of ourselves. It helps some of us to find out what we think. It is essential for the happiest companionship. One of the minor pleasures of affection is in the voicing of it. If you love your friend, says the song, tell him so. Talk helps one to get rid of the surplus enthusiasm that often blurs our ideas. Talk, as the sage says, relieves the tension of grief by dividing it. Talk is one of man's privileges, and with a little care it may be one of his blessings. The successful conversationalist is not the epigram maker, for sustained brilliance is blinding. The successful conversationalist says unusual things in a usual way. The successful conversationalist is not the man who does not think stupid things, but the man who does not say the stupid things he thinks. Silence is essential to every happy conversation. But not too much silence.

Too much silence may mean boredom or bewilderment. And it may mean scorn. For silence is an able weapon of pride. (80–81)

Mr. Blue teaches us that we act in mercy out of love of God, which is translated into love of neighbor.

8. It might come as a surprise that I am recommending Evelyn Waugh's *Helena* (1950) over what is pretty objectively his greatest work, the magnificent *Brideshead Revisited* (1945). Well, my recommendation is based solely on my great love of Saint Helena, who was the patroness of the parish to which I was assigned as a newly ordained priest. (Note that I've managed to work in a mention of the more famous *Brideshead* here, all the while introducing *Helena*!) It is said that Waugh himself believed that this was his best novel. It's the story of Helena, mother of the Emperor Constantine, and her quest to find the relics of the Lord's cross. It is a social commentary, with allegories to life in Britain during the time Waugh wrote it, while at the same time offering us a pious life of the great saint, Helena. And the character of Helena herself is wise and witty. Although not Waugh's usual style, this is a true pleasure to read.

9. François Mauriac's *A Woman of the Pharisees* (1941, translated into English in 1946) is a rich and complex novel that details the lives of rural French families in Bordeaux. Brigitte Pian is a pious and devout woman who can't help but involve herself in the lives of others. She is also a proud woman who, in her religious fervor, exerts control and domination over her family and others. Brigitte describes her spiritual life in this way:

> There had been a time when she was worried by the spiritual aridity that marked her relations with her God; but

since then she had read somewhere that it is as a rule the beginners on whom the tangible marks of Grace are showered, since it is only in that way that they can be extricated from the slough of this world and set upon the right path. The kind of insensitiveness that afflicted her was, she gathered, a sign that she had long ago emerged from those lower regions of the spiritual life where fervor is usually suspect. In this way her frigid soul was led on to glory in its own lack of warmth. (133)

Mauriac offers a very complex, thought-provoking text that can lead the reader to really examine himself or herself spiritually.

10. Brian Moore's *Black Robe* (1985) almost did not make this list, because many of his novels are very anticlerical. However, in many ways, this story of a Jesuit priest striving to bring the faith to Native Americans in sixteenth-century North America — all the while struggling with his own faith and sinfulness — can be seen alongside Graham Greene's *The Power and the Glory*. (Interestingly, Greene stated that Moore was his favorite contemporary novelist.) This is a tough book to read, but I think it illustrates the difficulties faced by the early Catholic missionaries in North America.

Appendix Four
Building a Library of the Fiction Classics of Western Civilization

This is a list of ten books that I believe would benefit every single person in the world, most especially Catholics! This list originates from a conversation that I had here at the seminary where I minister, the Pontifical North American College. I was speaking with my friend and colleague Father John Geary McDonald, who served as the Carl J. Peter Chair of Homiletics. We were speaking about the literary, historical, and artistic references that our seminarians make in general conversation at the lunch table, and even in homily *practica*. It struck both of us that, as highly intelligent as our seminarians are (and they really are!), many of them have come from a background where the classics of Western civilization were not deeply explored. I was asked to recommend classical fiction that our seminarians should be familiar with in order to become not only engaging preachers but also well-rounded men. I think that, as with the monks in the time of the Dark Ages, one of the roles of the priest is to help preserve learning. In our technological age, where endless information is available, fewer and fewer people have an interest in the classics, and everything focuses on sound bites, the priest (and indeed the Catholic Christian) needs to help preserve culture and learning. These choices are, again, mine, and therefore subjective. The early nineteenth-century German literary critic Friedrich Schlegel offers a good definition of a classic as "a writing that is never fully understood. But those that are educated and educate themselves must always want to learn more from it." Father David Tracy defines a classic as "those texts, events, images, persons, rituals and symbols which are assumed to disclose permanent possibilities of meaning and truth" (*The Analogical Imagination: Christian Theology and the Culture of Pluralism* [New York: Crossroad, 1981], 68). The classics have profoundly affected my understanding of the world. Please note that I am deliberately excluding works of Sacred Scripture, Sacred Tradition, the Church's Magisterium, the Catholic spiritual tradition, philosophy, or history from this list.

With no further ado, here is my list of fictional works from the Western literary tradition from which I believe all will benefit:

1. Homer's *The Odyssey* (end of the eighth century B.C.) is a profound work detailing the journey of Odysseus, and it is an excellent adventure story. An epic poem and a sequel to *The Iliad*, it is believed to be the second most ancient work of Western fiction. This summer, I had the joy of listening to it again on audiobook, which led me to think anew about how important this work, which I first read in high school, actually is. It is a hero's journey, and one might know it from one of its many adaptations, whether it be the Coen brothers' film *O Brother, Where Art Thou?* (2000) or Tim Burton's 2003 adaptation of Daniel Wallace's novel *Big Fish*. All Odysseus wants to do is get home to his wife, Penelope, and his son, Telemachus. Due to the fates, he is impeded in his journey home following the Trojan War. In his absence, suitors have lined up to woo his wife and take away his son's inheritance. With Greek gods influencing his fate, both positively and negatively, Odysseus and his crew encounter Circe, the enchantress; defeat the Cyclops; and escape from the land of the Lotus-Eaters. This is an epic poem depicting flawed heroes, homecoming, father-son relationships, loyalty, and friendship.

2. Dante Alighieri's *Divine Comedy*, an epic poem completed around 1320, is one of the greatest and most profound works of world literature. Divided into three parts, *Inferno*, *Purgatorio*, and *Paradiso*, the *Divine Comedy* tells the tale of Dante, a middle-aged man, who, with the aid of the Roman poet Virgil, pursues his muse, the lovely and elusive Beatrice. This journey takes Dante from the cold pit of hell, staring down a fat, bloated, pathetic Satan, to the heights of heaven. Deeply influenced by the Catholic philosophy and theology of his day, Dante's work has been described as "the *Summa* in verse."

3. *The Brothers Karamazov* by Fyodor Dostoevsky has been described as the greatest novel ever written. Completed in 1880, it is a tale of a Russian family that goes far beyond a "soap opera." Issues of faith and reason, doubt in the existence and providence of God, free will, and family are all part of this magnificent novel. Sadly, most of the film adaptations of this work have not been all that good. So do yourself a favor and read the book!

4. No list of classic literature would be complete without William Shakespeare. The noted American thinker Harold Bloom states that Shakespeare "invented the human" in the modern world. It is very difficult to pick one Shakespeare play as *the* one to read. I love so many of them for so many different reasons, from *The Tempest* to *Julius Caesar* to *Much Ado about Nothing*. However, most people consider Shakespeare's *Hamlet* (thought to have been written around 1599–1601) to be his best work. It is the tale of a son, Prince Hamlet of Denmark, who mourns the death of his father, the king, while his uncle Claudius has married his mother, Gertrude. Add to this the imminent attack by Prince Fortinbras of Norway and the love of Ophelia, and we can see why Hamlet is so moody and indecisive! The good thing is that this play has been performed well with many different actors in many different productions — from Laurence Olivier to Paul Giamatti, Benedict Cumberbatch, and even television's *Doctor Who* leads David Tennant and Christopher Eccleston.

5. T. S. Eliot's *Four Quartets* (1936–1942) is a collection of four poems, all of which deeply long for the transcendent. In fact, George Orwell, author of the dystopian novel *1984*, gave *Four Quartets* a bad review because he felt it was too religious! The four poems, "Burnt Norton," "East Coker," "The Dry Salvages," and "Little Gidding," are deeply beautiful reflections on life, death, and time. Although my favorite poem of T. S. Eliot is "The Love Song of J. Alfred Prufrock," I would suggest that the reader unfamiliar with the poet begin with this work. Interested listeners can go to YouTube and hear Eliot read his *Four Quartets* (https://www.youtube.com/watch?v=gB7BiC53ssk).

6. Russian writer Leo Tolstoy's 1878 work *Anna Karenina* is one of the most profound primers one could read on faith, family, and marriage. In this novel, Anna Karenina is a countess who has an affair with Count Alexei Kirillovich Vronsky. The count wants Anna to leave her husband, Alexei Alexandrovich Karenin, who is older than she is by twenty years. Alongside this story is the parallel story of Konstantin and his struggles with his family and his faith. This is not an easy or a quick read (it is around 1,000 pages), but it is well worth it. Although set in nineteenth-century Russia, it has universal themes to which all people can relate. Tolstoy begins the story with this line: "Happy families are all alike; every unhappy family is unhappy in its own way."

7. John Milton's *Paradise Lost* (1667; 1674) is an epic poem, written in blank verse, that details two narratives, one concerning Satan and the other concerning Adam and Eve. Satan's story is grand, beginning after the defeat of the fallen angels, who are now in Tartarus (hell). We hear accounts of the angelic war and the defeat of the fallen angels by the Son of God, as well as of the creation of the world. Satan willingly volunteers to go to the world and corrupt it. The story of Adam and Eve's Fall and expulsion from the Garden of Eden is recounted from their perspectives. Milton creates a charismatic Satan, filled with pride and arrogance; an Adam who is deeply infatuated with the far more intelligent Eve; and the heroic and all-powerful Son of God. *Paradise Lost* can be read as a commentary on England during the time of her civil war, but perhaps we might wish to read it as a biblical epic. Milton writes: "The mind is *its own place, and in it self / Can make a Heav'n of Hell, a Hell of Heav'n* (Book 1, lines 254–55; emphasis added).

8. *Don Quixote* by Miguel de Cervantes is one of the most influential pieces of literature in the world. Originally written in Spanish in two parts in 1605 and 1615, it is the story of the "Man of La Mancha," the nobleman Alonso Quixano, who, inspired by tales of the knights of old, names himself Don Quixote and sallies forth to find chivalric adventure and to win the hand of his Dulcinea. Aided by his "squire" (his neighbor, Sancho Panza), Don Quixote attacks windmills, believing them to be dragons. It is a fine book about honor and nobility, friendship, loyalty, women and men, fantasy, reality, madness, and, finally, how to treat people with respect. Cervantes writes: "When life itself seems lunatic, who knows where madness lies? Perhaps to be too practical is madness. To surrender dreams — this may be madness. Too much sanity may be madness — and maddest of all: to see life as it is, and not as it should be!"

9. Sir Arthur Conan Doyle's *Sherlock Holmes* is a very sentimental choice for me. Doyle wrote only four novels about the world's most famous consulting detective, the genius and, at times, misanthrope Sherlock Holmes, and his eager assistant, Dr. Watson: *A Study in Scarlet, The Sign of the Four, The Hound of the Baskervilles,* and *The Valley of Fear.* Most of Holmes and Watson's tales are found in the fifty-six short stories collected in five volumes, beginning with *The Adventures of Sherlock Holmes* and ending with *The Case-Book of Sherlock Holmes.* In my opinion, there is no fictional character greater than Holmes. I have read and reread these stories since I was a small boy, and it remains a thrill for me to catch up with my hero from 221B Baker Street. If you can read only a few stories, may I suggest "A Scandal in Bohemia," "The Adventure of the Speckled Band," "The Adventure of the Dancing Men, "The Red-Headed League," and "The Final Problem"?

10. I am embarrassed to include only one female author on this list; this is not a matter of sexism or misogyny but a product of my own reading style. Emily Brontë's 1847 novel *Wuthering Heights* is not everyone's "cup of tea," and having been forced to read it in high school, I was not too excited about it until I reread it many years later. The story of Heathcliff and Catherine is stark and Gothic, but it offers one of the most inspiring descriptions of identifying with one's beloved:

> "It is not," retorted she; "it is the best! The others were the satisfaction of my whims: and for Edgar's sake, too, to satisfy him. This is for the sake of one who compre-

hends in his person my feelings to Edgar and myself. I cannot express it; but surely you and everybody have a notion that there is or should be an existence of yours beyond you. What were the use of my creation, if I were entirely contained here? My great miseries in this world have been Heathcliff's miseries, and I watched and felt each from the beginning: my great thought in living is himself. If all else perished, and *he* remained, I should still continue to be; and if all else remained, and he were annihilated, the universe would turn to a mighty stranger: I should not seem a part of it. — My love for Linton is like the foliage in the woods: time will change it, I'm well aware, as winter changes the trees. My love for Heathcliff resembles the eternal rocks beneath: a source of little visible delight, but necessary. Nelly, I *am* Heathcliff! He's always, always in my mind: not as a pleasure, any more than I am always a pleasure to myself, but as my own being. So don't talk of our separation again: it is impracticable; and —' (chap. 9, 6)

In closing, remember this quote from Cervantes: "Finally, from so little sleeping and so much reading, his brain dried up and he went completely out of his mind." Don't be afraid! Get some sleep, but keep on reading.

Notes

Introduction
[1]*"Actiones Nostras"* is a traditional prayer before class.

Chapter 1
[1]See Gerald O'Collins, SJ, *Retrieving Fundamental Theology: The Three Styles of Contemporary Theology* (London: Geoffrey Chapman, 1993). Fr. O'Collins later updated his thoughts in his book *Rethinking Fundamental Theology* (New York: Oxford University Press, 2011) in chapter 13, "Theological Styles and Methods," 322–41. Additionally, Fr. O'Collins has written an excellent text, *The Bible for Theology: Ten Principles for the Theological Use of Scripture* (Mahwah, NJ/New York: Paulist, 1997), which is another useful tool for budding theologians.
[2]Anselm of Canterbury, *Cur Deus Homo*, Book 1, chap. 2, in *Patrologia Latina*, ed. J.-P. Migne, 158:362.
[3]Anselm, Preface to the *Proslogium*, available at Fordham University, "Medieval Sourcebook: Anselm (1033–1109): Proslogium," accessed November 15, 2019, https://sourcebooks.fordham.edu/basis/anselm-proslogium.asp#PREFACE.
[4]The Institute of the Brothers of the Christian Schools, more commonly known as the Christian Brothers, was founded in

France by Saint Jean-Baptiste de la Salle in 1679 and approved as a religious order by Pope Benedict XIII in 1725.

[5]Dorothy Day, *From Union Square to Rome* (Silver Spring, MD: Preservation of the Faith Press, 1938), chap. 1, http://dorothyday.catholicworker.org/articles/201.html.

[6]The *Catechism of the Catholic Church* reads: "The Church's faith precedes the faith of the believer who is invited to adhere to it. When the Church celebrates the sacraments, she confesses the faith received from the apostles — whence the ancient saying: *lex orandi, lex credendi* (or: *legem credendi lex statuat supplicandi* [the law of praying establishes the law of believing], according to Prosper of Aquitaine [5th cent.]). The law of prayer is the law of faith: the Church believes as she prays. Liturgy is a constitutive element of the holy and living Tradition" (1124).

[7]Here we might want to look at Mary Frohlich, "Thérèse of Lisieux: 'Doctor for the Third Millennium?'" *New Theology Review* 12, no. 3 (May 1999): 27–38. See also Father Frederick L. Miller, STD, *The Trial of Faith of St. Therese of Lisieux* (Staten Island, NY: Alba House, 1998). Both offer a remarkable introduction to exactly why this young nun should be considered a Doctor of the Church.

[8]Thérèse of Lisieux, *Story of a Soul: The Autobiography of St. Thérèse of Lisieux*, ed. T. N. Taylor (London: Burns, Oates & Washbourne, 1912).

[9]Ibid.

[10]"The Life of Saint Thérèse of Lisieux," Vatican.va.

[11]Aidan Nichols, OP, *The Shape of Catholic Theology* (Edinburgh: T&T Clark, 1991), 15.

[12]Father Robert Imbelli, in the introduction to his excellent text *Rekindling the Christic Imagination: Theological Meditations for the New Evangelization* (Collegeville, MN: Liturgical Press, 2014), brings this point home powerfully for his readers, espe-

cially on pages xviii–xv.

[13]According to Gerald O'Collins, SJ, and Edward G. Farrugia, SJ, positive theology is "a branch of theology that deals with historical data and particular facts (drawn from the Bible and tradition to determine the doctrines Christians believe), as opposed to natural theology, which treats of universal religious principles known from reason. Today positive theology seldom appears among the schemes for dividing the whole field of theology: its place has often been taken by historical theology." *A Concise Dictionary of Theology*, rev. ed. (Mahwah, NJ/ New York: Paulist Press, 2000), 207.

Chapter 2

[1]John Paul II, *Pastores Dabo Vobis*; and United States Conference of Catholic Bishops, *Program of Priestly Formation* (5th ed.), 2006.

[2]There's a great amount to unpack in this statement. *A Concise Dictionary of Theology* defines "analogy" as "the use of a common term to designate realities that are both similar and dissimilar with regard to the same point (e.g., 'love,' as predicated of God and human beings." It goes on to explain that "analogy is to be distinguished from (a) the case of equivocal terms, i.e., terms that are the same but designate totally dissimilar realities (e.g., *pen* as an enclosure for cows and as writing instrument); and (b) the case of univocal or perfectly synonymous terms, i.e., different terms that refer to an identical reality (e.g., *king* and *sovereign* for the male hereditary ruler of an independent state)." As for nominalism, it is an idea that names for things cannot truly describe reality. *A Concise Dictionary of Theology* states that for a nominalist, "every substance is irreducibly individual; there are no common natures; and universal concepts exist only in the mind." (It is apparent that a nominalist view of God and the sacraments will produce

substantial theological issues.) O'Collins and Farrugia, "Nominalism," *Concise Dictionary of Theology*, 176.

[3]Modernity is a period of history largely thought to have been ushered in by René Descartes's ideas, which have ushered in a new way of being, an age of a dualism between one's mind and one's body. For a good understanding of post-modernity, please see Michael Paul Gallagher, SJ's *Clashing Symbols: An Introduction to Faith and Culture*, rev. ed. (London: Darton, Longman, Todd, 2003), especially chapter 8, "The Post-Modern Situation — Friend or Foe?," 98–114.

[4]O'Collins and Farrugia, "Metaphysics," *Concise Dictionary of Theology*, 156.

[5]For some fine introductory books on how to understand philosophy, I suggest the following texts: Peter Kreeft, *Summa of the Summa* (San Francisco: Ignatius Press, 2011); Mortimer J. Adler, *Aristotle for Everybody: Difficult Thought Made Easy* (New York: Touchstone, 1997 [reprint]); Mortimer J. Adler, *Ten Philosophical Mistakes* (New York: Touchstone, 1997 [reprint]); Edward Feser, *Five Proofs of the Existence of God* (San Francisco: Ignatius Press, 2017); and Brian Clayton and Douglas Kries, *Two Wings: Integrating Faith and Reason* (San Francisco: Ignatius Press, 2018).

[6]Second Vatican Council, *Dei Verbum*, accessed April 20, 2020, Vatican.va, par. 11.

[7]These divisions within the Old Testament come from the Jewish people themselves.

[8]This number of books comes from the Catholic tradition: The Fathers of the Church, such as St. Athanasius in his *Paschal Epistle* (A.D. 367), as well as the Synods of Hippo (393) and Carthage I and II (397 and 419). The letter of Pope St. Innocent I in 405 also officially listed these books. The Council of Florence in 1442 restated this listing, as did the Council of Trent in its *Decree on Sacred Books and on Traditions to be Received*

(1546), confirming that Catholics accept the seven "deutero-canonical" books — Tobit, Judith, Wisdom, Sirach, Baruch, I and II Maccabees, and Esther. This is also affirmed in the *Catechism of the Catholic Church*, which states: "It was by the apostolic Tradition that the Church discerned which writings are to be included in the list of the sacred books. This complete list is called the canon of Scripture. It includes 46 books for the Old Testament (45 if we count Jeremiah and Lamentations as one) and 27 for the New" (CCC 120). In total, the Old Testament contains Genesis, Exodus, Leviticus, Numbers, Deuteronomy, Joshua, Judges, Ruth, 1 and 2 Samuel, 1 and 2 Kings, 1 and 2 Chronicles, Ezra and Nehemiah, Tobit, Judith, Esther, 1 and 2 Maccabees, Job, Psalms, Proverbs, Ecclesiastes, the Song of Songs, the Wisdom of Solomon, Sirach (Ecclesiasticus), Isaiah, Jeremiah, Lamentations, Baruch, Ezekiel, Daniel, Hosea, Joel, Amos, Obadiah, Jonah, Micah, Nahum, Habakkuk, Zephaniah, Haggai, Zachariah and Malachi. The New Testament contains the Gospels according to Matthew, Mark, Luke, and John; the Acts of the Apostles; the Letters of St. Paul to the Romans, 1 and 2 Corinthians, Galatians, Ephesians, Philippians, Colossians, 1 and 2 Thessalonians, 1 and 2 Timothy, Titus, and Philemon; the Letter to the Hebrews; the Letters of James, 1 and 2 Peter, 1, 2, and 3 John, and Jude; and Revelation (the Apocalypse).

[9]O'Collins and Farrugia, "Tradition," *Concise Dictionary of Theology*, 270.

Chapter 3

[1]O'Collins and Farrugia define "eschatology" as "That branch of systematic theology which studies God's final kingdom as expressed by its OT [Old Testament] preparations (e.g., the messianic hopes), the preaching of Jesus, and the teaching of the NT [New Testament] church." See "Eschatology," *A Concise*

Dictionary of Theology, 79.

[2]According to O'Collins and Farrugia, ecclesiology is "that branch of theology which systematically reflects on the origin, nature, distinguishing characteristics, and mission of the Church." "Ecclesiology," *Concise Dictionary of Theology*, 71.

[3]For more explanation, please see Jean-Pierre Torrell, OP, *Saint Thomas Aquinas*, trans. Robert Royal, 2 vols. (Washington, DC: Catholic University of America Press, 2005 and 2003).

[4]Thomas Aquinas, *Summa Theologiae*, I, q.1, a.1.

[5]Jorge Mario Bergoglio and Abraham Skorka, *On Heaven and Earth*, trans. Alejandro Bermudez and Howard Goodman (New York: Random House, 2013), xiv.

Chapter 4

[1]C. S. Lewis, *A Preface to Paradise Lost* (Oxford University Press, 1960), 1.

[2]J. J. Mueller, *What Are They Saying about the Theological Method?* (Ramsey, NJ: Paulist Press, 1984), 2.

[3]Ross A. Shecterle, *The Theology of Avery Dulles 1980–1994: Symbolic Mediation*, Roman Catholic Studies vol. 8 (Lewiston/Queenston/Lampeter: Edward Mellen Press, 1996), xix.

[4]Ignatius of Antioch, *Epistle to the Smyrnaeans*, chap. 1–2, in *Apostolic Fathers*, ed. J. B. Lightfoot (London: Macmillan, 1889), II/2: 289–293; SCh 10, 154–56.

[5]Second Vatican Council, *Lumen Gentium*, accessed April 20, 2020, Vatican.va, par. 63.

[6]See, among other works, Joseph Ratzinger and Hans Urs von Balthasar, *Mary, the Church at the Source*, trans. Adrian Walker (San Francisco: Ignatius Press, 2005).

[7]Edward D. Gratsch, *Aquinas' Summa* (Staten Island, NY: Alba House, 1983), ix.

Chapter 5

[1]Collect of the Mass of the Feast of Saint Luke (October 18), *The Roman Missal.*

[2]Robert Sokolowski, *Christian Faith & Human Understanding: Studies on the Eucharist, Trinity, and the Human Person* (Washington, DC: Catholic University of America Press, 2006), 94.

[3]Please see https://www.theologicalcollege.org/sulpician -tradition/. The Society of San Sulpice, a community of diocesan priests founded in Paris in 1641 by Father Olier, has a long and rich tradition of forming men for the diocesan priesthood. The Sulpicians came to the United States at the request of the first American bishop, John Carroll, in 1791 to establish the first seminary in the new country, Saint Mary's Seminary in Baltimore, Maryland.

[4]The United States Conference of Catholic Bishops website gives a beautiful understanding of what the Liturgy of the Hours is. It states: "The Liturgy of the Hours, also known as the Divine Office or the Work of God (*Opus Dei*), is the daily prayer of the Church, marking the hours of each day and sanctifying the day with prayer. The Hours are a meditative dialogue on the mystery of Christ, using Scripture and prayer. At times the dialogue is between the Church or individual soul and God; at times it is a dialogue among the members of the Church; and at times it is even between the Church and the world. The Divine Office 'is truly the voice of the Bride herself addressed to her Bridegroom. It is the very prayer which Christ himself together with his Body addresses to the Father.' (SC 84) The dialogue is always held, however, in the presence of God and using the words and wisdom of God." See http://www. usccb.org/prayer-and-worship/liturgy-of-the-hours/index.cfm. Those in the clerical state (deacons, priests, and bishops) are obliged to pray the Divine Office daily (see Code of Canon Law

276).

[5]As an aid in getting to know the Fathers a bit better, I suggest two fine books. The first is by Father Boniface Ramsey, *Beginning to Read the Fathers*, rev. ed. (Mahwah, NJ: Paulist Press, 2012); and the second is Christopher A. Hall's *Reading Scripture with the Church Fathers* (Westmont, IL: InterVarsity Press, 1998).

[6]The *ressourcement* period lasted roughly from the 1920s to the 1960s and had a major impact on the theology of the Second Vatican Council. It was first called *nouvelle théologie* by Réginald Marie Garrigou-Lagrange, who declared "The *nouvelle théologie* will lead us back to modernism." [See "La nouvelle théologie où va-t-elle?" *Angelicum* 23 (146): 143.] This *nouvelle théologie* had major proponents, including Henri de Lubac, Marie-Dominique Chenu, Louis Bouyer, and Jean Daniélou. Congar, a Dominican professor at Le Saulchoir school of theology in Paris, was an early ecumenist and ecclesiologist. His early works included *Chrétiens désunis: Principes d'un 'oecuménisme' catholique* (1937). Chenu, another Dominican, actively studied Thomas Aquinas's theology within its proper historical context and was reprimanded for his publication of *Le Saulchoir: Une école de la théologie* (1937), among other works. Oratorian Louis Boyer brought *ressourcement* to liturgical studies and is considered a founder in the liturgical reform movement. Daniélou, a Jesuit, insisted in his writings on the importance of the patristic writers for contemporary theology.

The *nouvelle théologie* accepted the neo-Scholastic principle of the sevenfold *loci proprii* (proper sources) of theology, as articulated by Melchior Cano (1509–1560) — namely, Scripture, Tradition, the Church (in its faith awareness), the ecumenical councils, the Fathers, the Scholastics, and the *ecclesia Romana* (the pope) (see Nichols, *The Shape of Catholic Theology*, 318). However, the proponents of *nouvelle théologie* also focused on secondary sources of theology, the *loci alieni*, areas long ignored by neo-Scholasticism — namely, history, reason, and philosophy. There were four principle characteristics of the *nouvelle théologie* of which one should be aware: its French language; its use of history; its use of positive theology — looking to the liturgy, patristic writings, and Sacred Scripture; and its hypercritical attitude toward neo-Scholasticism. See J. Mettepenningen, *Nouvelle Théologie — New Theology: Inheritor of Modernism, Precursor of Vatican II* (Edinburgh: T&T Clark, 2010).

[7]C. S. Lewis, "Introduction to Athanasius' *On the Incarnation*" (1944), ReformedLiterature.com, accessed January 6, 2020, https://www.bhmc.org.uk/uploads/9/1/7/7/91773502 /lewis-incarnation-intro.pdf.

[8]If you would like a good anthology of the Fathers, try *The Early Christian Fathers: A Selection from the Writings of the Fathers from St. Clement of Rome to St. Athanasius*, ed. and trans. Henry Bettenson (Oxford University Press, 1969) and Bettenson's *The Later Christian Fathers: A Selection from the Writings of the Fathers from St. Cyril of Jerusalem to St. Leo the Great* (Oxford University Press, 1973).

[9]Cyprian, "Epistle 1, To Donatus," trans. Robert E. Wallis, in *The Writings of Cyprian, Bishop of Carthage*, ed. Alexander Roberts and James Donaldson, vol. 1 (Edinburgh: T&T Clark, 1868).

[10]I highly recommend the Ignatius Critical Edition of *The Confessions* (2012), edited by Jesuit Father David Meconi and translated by Benedictine Sister Maria Boulding.

[11]Irenaeus, *Adversus Haereses*, Book 4, chap. 20.

[12]Gregory Nazianzen, "Oration 43 — *In Laudem Basilii Magni*" (In Praise of Basil the Great).

[13]Cyril of Alexandria, "Letter II to Nestorius."

[14]Henri de Lubac, *Medieval Exegesis*, trans. Mark Sebanc, vol.

1, *The Four Senses of Scripture* (Grand Rapids, MI: Eerdmans, 1998), 1.

[15] Benedict XVI (Joseph Ratzinger), *Jesus of Nazareth: From the Baptism in the Jordan to the Transfiguration,* trans. Adrian T. Walker (New York: Doubleday, 2007), 78.

[16] Ignatius of Antioch, *The Epistle of Ignatius to the Philadelphians,* chap. 5.

[17] Stephen Beale, "Which Church Fathers Most Influenced St. Thomas Aquinas?" *National Catholic Register,* February 8, 2018.

Chapter 6

[1] John Courtney Murray (1904–1967) was a priest of the New York Province of the Society of Jesus. After earning his doctorate (S.T.D.) at the Pontifical Gregorian University in Rome, Father Murray went on to teach for many years at Woodstock Theological Seminary in Maryland and served as an editor of both *America* magazine and *Theological Studies.* Father Murray was an influential figure as a *peritus* (theological advisor) at Vatican II and was one of the main architects of Vatican II's *Dignitatis Humanae* (Declaration on Religious Freedom) (1965).

[2] James Hennesey, *American Catholics: A History of the Roman Catholic Community in the United States,* foreword by John Tracy Ellis (New York/Oxford: Oxford University Press, 1981), 164.

[3] James Hennesey, "The Baltimore Council of 1866: An American Syllabus," *Records of the American Catholic Historical Society of Philadelphia* 76 (1965): 161–65.

[4] I refer to such thinkers as Alfred Loisy (1857–1940), George Tyrell (1861–1909), Ernesto Buonaiuti (1881–1946) and Maude Petre (1863–1942). Loisy, from France, was the author of *L'Évangile et l'église* (1902) and was excommunicated in 1908;

Tyrell, from Ireland, was the author, among many other works, of *Hard Sayings: A Selection of Meditations and Studies* (1899), and was expelled from the Society of Jesus in 1906; Buonaiuti, from Italy, was a prolific writer who wrote *Storia del cristianesimo* (1942–1943) and was excommunicated in 1925; Petre, from England, was a member of the religious congregation of the Daughters of the Heart of Mary and wrote *Catholicism and Independence: Being Studies in Spiritual Liberty* (1907) and *Modernism: Its Failure and Its Fruits* (1918).

[5] See O'Collins and Farrugia, "Americanism," *Concise Dictionary of Theology*, 7. They define it as such: "An ill-defined nineteenth-century movement among Catholics in the U.S.A. who were open to the best ideals of American Puritanism, the Enlightenment, incipient ecumenism, and contemporary culture. … Some themes of Americanism, such as religious liberty, were later vindicated in Vatican II."

[6] Leo XIII, *Aeterni Patris, Acta Apostolicae Sedis* 12 (1879), 98.

[7] Jared Wicks, *Introduction to Theological Method* (Casale Monferrato: Piemme Press, 1994), 25.

[8] Ibid.

[9] See John Michael McDermott, "The Collapse of the Manualist Tradition," *Faith Magazine* (January–February 2014), https://www.faith.org.uk/article/january-february-2014-the-collapse-of-the-manualist-tradition. He writes:

> The numerous virtues of manualist theology can scarcely be denied. … Presenting the faith clearly to students, it distinguished essentials from theological speculation and legitimate pluralism. Thus the unity of faith was readily perceived and preserved. Continuity from the basic catechism to its most elaborate theological expansion for seminarians also facilitated learning. Since most manuals were composed in Latin, this universal language daily reminded students that the unity of faith encompassed

the whole world and was centered on Rome. Its method
likewise emphasized continuity with Scripture, Tradition
and magisterial pronouncements since all these sources of revelation and authentic teaching were listed and
learned. This allowed priests readily to answer questions
from believers and respond to criticism from Protestants
and non-believers. The perception of the faith's inherent
intelligibility was available even to intellects not especially
endowed with speculative genius. ... The witness of the
Church was clear in faith and morals, as might be expected from an institution divinely established and promised
perpetual duration.

[10]This is exemplified by the theology of Édouard Hugon
(1867–1929), Réginald Marie Garrigou-Lagrange (1877–1964),
and Martin Grabmann (1875–1949) as the seemingly approved
"Roman Catholic Theology." All three of these neo-Thomists
were connected to the Pontifical University of Saint Thomas
Aquinas (the Angelicum) in Rome. The Dominican Édouard
Hugon is best known as the author, along with the Jesuit Gui-
do Mattiussi, of the manual *The 24 Thomistic Theses* (1941); the
Dominican Réginald Marie Garrigou-Lagrange was a prolific
and widely read author and is most famous for his text *Les trois
ages de la vie intérieure* (1938); Martin Grabmann's chief work
was *Thomas von Aquin: Eine Einführung in seine Persönlichkeit
und Gedankenwelt* (1912).
[11]Tracey Rowland, *Ratzinger's Faith: The Theology of Pope Benedict XVI* (New York: Oxford University Press, 2008), 18.
[12]Marie-Dominique Chenu, "L'Interprète de saint Thomas
d'Aquin," in *Étienne Gilson et nous: la philosophie et son his-
toire*, ed. M. Couratier (Paris: Vrin, 1980), 43–44, as cited in
Rowland, *Ratzinger's Faith*, 19.
[13]Jürgen Mettepenningen, *Nouvelle Théologie — New Theology:*

Inheritor of Modernism, Precursor of Vatican II (London: T&T Clark, 2010), 12.

[14]*Lamentabili Sane Exitu* was written by the Holy Office and approved by the pope in 1907. It attempted to address exegesis of Sacred Scripture and how best to interpret dogma. *Pascendi Dominici Gregis* was an encyclical by Pius X that directly addressed and condemned the heresy of modernism.

[15]*Mystici Corporis Christi* (On the Mystical Body of Christ, 1943) was an encyclical that addressed the nature of the Church, an entity both visible and invisible. It spoke of the Church as the "Body of Christ," a return to a patristic notion; addressed the role of the bishops and laity; and condemned many serious dangers of the time, such as nationalism, racism, and euthanasia. *Mediator Dei* ("Mediator of God": On the Sacred Liturgy, 1947) defined the nature of sacred theology and suggested new directions for the role of the faithful. *Divino Afflante Spiritu* (Inspired by the Holy Spirit, 1943) was an encyclical that encouraged the use of modern methods of Scripture scholarship such as textual criticism and knowledge of the Bible in the original languages.

[16]John XXIII, *Humanae Salutis*; English translation provided by Joseph Komonchak, accessed January 6, 2020, https://jakomonchak.files.wordpress.com/2011/12/humanae-salutis.pdf.

[17]Second Vatican Council, *Gaudium et Spes*, accessed January 6, 2020, Vatican.va, para. 4.

[18]John XXIII, *Mater et Magistra*, accessed January 6, 2020, Vatican.va, par. 236.

[19]Peter Hebblethwaite, *Paul VI: The First Modern Pope* (Mahwah, NJ: Paulist Press, 2018; first edition 1993).

[20]Paul VI, private note, 1978, written shortly before his death, as quoted in Cahal B. Daly, *Steps on My Pilgrim Journey* (Dublin: Veritas, 1998), 177.

[21]Paul VI, *Humanae Vitae*, accessed April 20, 2020, Vatican.va,

para. 9.

[22]For greater context on this change of heart, please see Joseph Ratzinger, *Introduction to Christianity* (San Francisco: Ignatius Press, 2008; first edition 1968). To truly ascertain the meaning of the Communio school, please consult the following: Joseph Ratzinger, "Communio: A Program," *Communio: International Catholic Review* 19 (Fall 1992): 436–49; and Hans Urs von Balthasar, *The Moment of Christian Witness* (San Francisco: Ignatius Press, 2012; first edition 1968).

[23]O'Collins and Farrugia, "Christology from Above," *Concise Dictionary of Theology*, 42.

[24]For more information, see Tracey Rowland, *Culture and the Thomist Tradition after Vatican II* (London: Routledge, 2003). For an example of *ressourcement* Thomism, please consult *Ressourcement Thomism: Sacred Doctrine, the Sacraments, and the Moral Life*, ed. Reinhard Hütter and Matthew Levering (Washington, DC: Catholic University of America Press, 2010). Another excellent study of the variety of approaches to Thomism can be found in Fergus Kerr, *After Aquinas: Versions of Thomism* (London: Blackwell, 2002).

[25]According to O'Collins and Farrugia, personalism is "a philosophy centered on the unique value of human persons. … It opposes totalitarian ideologies …, behaviorism, and any psychology that understands human beings as case studies to be interpreted simply in terms of their functions and reactions. … True personalism excludes any selfish individualism bent on furthering one's own 'interests' at the expense of others." "Personalism," *Concise Dictionary of Theology*, 199.

[26]*Redemptor Hominis* was an encyclical released on March 4, 1979, that discussed some of the major problems facing the world at the time. The solution, according to the pope, was to be found in a greater understanding of the human person and a greater understanding of Jesus Christ. 1984's apostolic letter

Salvifici Doloris was written to discuss our "partnership in suffering" with the Lord Jesus. In *Salvifici Doloris* 19, John Paul II writes: "In bringing about the Redemption through suffering, Christ *has* also *raised human suffering to the level of the Redemption.* Thus each man, in his suffering, can also become a sharer in the redemptive suffering of Christ."

[27]George A. Kelly, *Keeping the Church Catholic with John Paul II* (San Francisco: Ignatius Press, 1993).

[28]See Benedict XVI, "General Audience, April 27, 2005," Vatican.va.

[29]Joseph Ratzinger, *The Spirit of the Liturgy*, trans. John Saward (San Francisco: Ignatius Press, 2000).

[30]Juan Carlos Scannone, "Papa Francesco e la teologia del popolo," *La Civiltà Cattolica* 3930 (March 15, 2014): 571–90.

[31]Ibid., 572–73.

[32]Ibid., 576.

[33]Francis, "Meeting with the Authorities in Seoul," accessed January 6, 2020, Vatican.va.

[34]Gerard Whelan, "Pope Francis, Bernard Lonergan, and Contextual Theology," 5, citing Gustavo Gutiérrez, "The Preferential Option for the Poor at Aparecida," 71–92, in *Aparecida: Quo Vadis?*, ed. Richard Pelton, (Scranton, PA: University of Scranton, 2008).

[35]Francesca Ambrogetti and Sergio Rubin, *Pope Francis: Conversations with Jorge Bergoglio: His Life in His Own Words* (New York: New American Library/Penguin, 2014), 74.

[36]Pope Francis as quoted by John Navone in the afterword of *Triumph through Failure: A Theology of the Cross* (Eugene, OR: Wipf & Stock, 2014), 181.

[37]John P. Cush, "Encyclical Was the Work of Four Hands," *The Tablet*, July 17, 2013.

[38]Scannone, "Papa Francesco," 583–85.

[39]See Gerard Whelan, "Pope Francis and Lonergan Studies: A

Providential Moment?" (unpublished manuscript), 8.

[40]Ibid., 9.

[41]Charles J. Chaput, OFM Cap, "'Amoris Laetitia' and the Nature of Mercy," CatholicPhilly.com, November 8, 2017, http://catholicphilly.com/2017/11/homilies-speeches/amoris-laetitia-and-the-nature-of-mercy/.

Chapter 7

[1]Rudolf Otto, *The Idea of the Holy: An Inquiry into the Non-Rational Factor in the Idea of the Divine and its Relation to the Rational*, trans. John W. Harvey (Oxford University Press, 1923).

[2]CatholicCulture.org defines social sin as "The sinfulness of society into which a person is born. Its premise is that modern socialization and collectivization have immersed everyone in other people's values and moral actions to an unprecedented degree." https://www.catholicculture.org/culture/library/dictionary/index.cfm?id=36530.

[3]Joseph Ratzinger, "Intervention for the Presentation of the Apostolic Letter in the Form of Motu Proprio *Misericordia Dei*," accessed April 20, 2020, Vatican.va.

[4]Robert Kysar, *John, the Maverick Gospel* (Louisville, KY: Westminster John Knox Press, 1993).

[5]Pew Research Center, "What Americans Know about Religion," July 23, 2019, https://www.pewforum.org/2019/07/23/what-americans-know-about-religion/.

[6]Gregory A. Smith, "Just One-Third of U.S. Catholics Agree with Their Church That Eucharist Is Body, Blood of Christ," Pew Research Center, *Fact Tank*, August 5, 2019, https://www.pewresearch.org/fact-tank/2019/08/05/transubstantiation-eucharist-u-s-catholics/.

[7]"What Is the Eucharist?" *Word on Fire*, accessed April 13, 2020, https://www.wordonfire.org/presence/.

[8]Robert Barron, "Bishop Barron on Catholics Misunderstanding the Eucharist," August 6, 2019, https://youtu.be/0yTGlYCIvks.
[9]Georges Bernanos, *The Diary of a Country Priest*, trans. Pamela Morris (Classica Libris, 2019; French original, 1936).

Chapter 8

[1]Bernard J. F. Lonergan, *Method in Theology* (London: Darton, Longman, and Todd, 1972), 20, 53, 55, 231, 302.
[2]Donald E. Pelotte, *John Courtney Murray: Theologian in Conflict* (New York: Paulist Press, 1976), 21n1. Donald Pelotte notes that an excerpt of Murray's thesis was found in John Courtney Murray, "The Root of Faith: The Doctrine of M. J. Scheeben," *Theological Studies* 9 (March 1948): 20–46. Scheeben (1835–1888), a dogmatist focused on theological epistemology and first principles and interested less in apologetics than in theological reflection, would remain an important influence on Murray's theology. See Bernd Groth, "Scheeben, Matthias Joseph," in *The Dictionary of Fundamental Theology*, ed. René Latourelle and Rino Fisichella (New York: Crossroad, 1994), 962–63.
[3]For those looking for a great introduction to Scheeben, Michael Barber has a wonderful post: "Matthias Scheeben on the Mysteries of Christianity (Part 1)." I am indebted to Barber's fine synthesis for my own initial understanding of Scheeben.
[4]Matthias J. Scheeben, *Die Herrlichkeiten der Göttlichen Gnade* (*The Magnificence of Divine Grace*) (Freiburg im Breisgau: Herder, 1863), 3; as quoted in Scheeben, *The Holy Spirit*, compiled by Friedrich Fuchs, SVD, trans. Leon Jungblut, SVD (Allahabad, India: St. Paul Publications, 1974), 152–53.
[5]Matthias J. Scheeben, *The Mysteries of Christianity* (New York: Crossroad, 2008).
[6]Quoted in *L'Osservatore Romano*, March 11–12, 1935.
[7]Scheeben, *The Mysteries of Christianity* (St. Louis: B. Herder

Books, 1946), 21.
[8]Ibid.
[9]Ibid.

Postscript

[1]Francis, "Address for the Conclusion of the Third Extraordinary General Assembly of the Synod of Bishops," accessed April 20, 2020, Vatican.va.

About the Author

Born in Brooklyn, New York, Father John Patrick Cush is a priest of the Diocese of Brooklyn. Ordained in 1998, he earned a doctorate in sacred theology (STD) from the Pontifical Gregorian University in Rome, Italy, with a specialization in fundamental theology. Father Cush currently serves as academic dean and as a formation advisor at the Pontifical North American College, Vatican City State. He is also an adjunct assistant professor of theology at the Pontifical Gregorian University and an adjunct professor of church history at the Pontifical University of the Holy Cross. Father Cush writes regularly for the *National Catholic Register*, *The Tablet*, *The Evangelist*, and *Homiletics and Pastoral Review*. He has served as a parish priest, a high school teacher, and a censor of books for his diocese.

Made in the USA
Las Vegas, NV
19 September 2022

55585818R00128